READ

LIMIT

30 mph

Johnny A Palmer Jr.

(The book of Song of Solomon outlined, plus)

CONTENT

INTRODUCTION to the Book...

COURTSHIP...

Shulamite's Desire– Lips; Love; Lotion; Longing.

Shulamite is Described – Fairest; Follower; Filly; Fragrance;
Facial features; beautiful Forest; Flower; Fruit tree; Flag; Fatigue; Force; Fast-forward; Favored; Fortress; little Foxes; Faithfulness; Frantic search; Finds him.

CONSUMMATION...

Foreplay – Brown eyes; Black hair; Beautiful teeth; Bright lips; Bull neck; Breasts; no Blemishes; Beckons; Begins; Garden Between her legs.

Forbidden no more – two Become one; God's Blessing.

CONFLICT...

Her Questionable slumber – Awake; Aware.

Her sexual thirst Quenched – He Comes; Calls; Continues; Complements; Complains.

She Quenches his efforts

Her Quantum leap

Her Quick departure

Her Quest

Her Quandary

The Question – Charge; Challenge;

His Qualifications – Radiance; Ruddy; Rare; Royalty; Raven; Rivers; Rugged; Reddish; Rippling; Ripped; Robust; Rugged; Romantic; well Rounded.

Her Queen answer

The Queen

A Quiet garden

ReQuest to gaze

CONQUEST OF LOVE

Love always *Expresses* itself – Feet; Form; Facial features; Focus; Finding a getaway; Freely.

Love always *Experiences* obstacles

Love is *Exacting*

Love *Excels*

Love is *Exclusive*

Love is *Exciting*

Love is a Divine *Expression*

Love cannot be *Extinguished*

Love is beyond *Expensive*

Love is *Exemplary*

Love lives in *Expectancy*

INTRODUCTION

I never liked long introductions, few people bother to read them anyway. But I just wanted to begin with a warning – this book is only for those 30 years old – or older! That's right! The Jewish leaders taught that young people should not read it until they were 30 years old. Well, the title is designed to get people's attention, and if you're under 30 years old I won't tell if you take a peek. The truth is, this book like all Scripture is inspired by God and therefore a great blessing to anyone who reads it (2 Tim. 3:16). So there it is, a brief and unenlightening introduction – see that wasn't so bad.

Oh, one more quick note for those self-righteous knot heads who will be offended by the content of this book – just don't buy the book! And don't send me your hate mail; take it up with God, the author of this book!

CHAPTER ONE

INTRODUCTION TO THE SONG OF SOLOMON

Charles Stanley, "Does God have anything to say to us about love; sex; and intimacy? For many people the words "romance" and "Bible" conjure up a long list of religious "Thou shall not's." But God never intended for us to view love, in a negative way. He created us in love, and for love, and for that reason, the Bible has a great deal to say about romantic love. In fact, it often uses pictures of human love, to help us understand God's love for us."

I have avoided preaching through this book for many years, but I finally decided to take a stab at it.

INTRODUCTION to the Song of Solomon

Song of Solomon 1:1 — How did a sensual book like this get in the Bible?

- Problem 1 - The Bible condemns the lust of the flesh and sensuality (Rom. 6:6; Gal. 5:16-21; 1 John 2:16). Yet this love song is filled with sensual expressions and sexual overtures (cf. 1:2; 2:5; 3:1; 4:5).

Solution 1 - The Bible does not condemn sex, but only perverted sex. God created sex (Gen. 1:27), and He ordained that it should be enjoyed within the bonds of a monogamous marriage and in a relationship of love. The Scriptures declare:

"Rejoice with the wife of your youth. As a loving deer and a graceful doe, let her breasts satisfy you at all times; and always be enraptured with her love" (Prov. 5:18-19)

After warning against those who forbid marriage (1 Tim. 4:3), the apostle declares that "every creature of God is good" (v. 4), and he goes on to speak of the God "who gives us richly all things to enjoy" (6:17). Hebrews insists that "marriage is honorable among all, and the bed undefiled; but fornicators and adulterers God will judge" (Heb. 13:4).

God realizes that normal people will have sexual desires, but He adds, "Nevertheless, because of sexual immorality, let each man have his own wife, and let each woman have her own husband" (1 Cor. 7:2). So, sex itself is not sinful, nor is sexual desires. God created them and intends that they be enjoyed within the loving bonds of a monogamous marriage.

The Song of Solomon is a divinely authoritative example of how sensual love should be expressed in marriage.

PROBLEM 2 - Some question whether this book should be in the Bible, claiming that some rabbis rejected it. Was it always a part of the Jewish Scriptures?

Solution 2 - From the very earliest times, this book was part of the Jewish canon. Centuries after it was accepted into the canon of Scriptures, the school of Shammai (a.d. 1st century) expressed doubt about its inspiration, but the view of Rabbi Akiba ben Joseph (c. a.d. 50-132) prevailed when he declared:

"God forbid!—No man in Israel ever disputed about the Song of Songs... for all the ages are not worthy the day on which the Song of Songs was given to Israel; for all the writings are holy, but the Song of Songs is the Holiest of Holies" (See Geisler and Nix, A General Introduction to the Bible, Moody Press, 1986, 259).

Problem 3 - Evangelical Christians defend the literal interpretation of the Bible. They insist that it should be taken in its normal, historical-grammatical sense, not in some hidden, mystical, or allegorical sense.

To do so in the Gospels, for example, leads to liberalism, denying the historicity of the life, death, and resurrection of Christ. However, many evangelicals do not take the Song of Solomon literally, but give it an allegorical or spiritual meaning. Is this not inconsistent?

Solution 3 - There are three basic interpretations of the Song of Solomon: the literal, the allegorical, and the typical.

First, there is a literal interpretation. According to this view, it is a literal story about King Solomon and his love for his wife and her love for him, although scholars differ over just which of his 700 wives and 300 concubines (1 Kings 11:3) this might be. Some say it was "the daughter of Pharaoh" (1 Kings 11:1). Others suggest it was a lowly maiden known as the Shulamite. But all who take it literally insist that it is about the historical King Solomon and a love affair he had with a woman. They insist, then, that the book is intended to extol the beauty, purity, and sanctity of marriage.

Second, others take an allegorical interpretation of the book, shying away from the more sensuously descriptive parts of the story. They prefer to see a deeper meaning, such as Yahweh's love for His people Israel (cf. Hosea) or, more broadly, God's love for His people in general.

Third, many Christians opt for a typical interpretation of this canticle, seeing in it the prefiguration or type of Christ and His love for the church (cf. Eph. 5:28-32). This view also denies that the book should be taken in a literal sense, insisting rather on a deeper spiritual meaning.

Whatever application this love story may have, to God's relation to His people, or Christ's love for His church, it seems better to insist on a literal interpretation for the following two basic reasons:

First, it is inconsistent to allegorize this story and insist on taking the Gospels and other parts of Scripture literally.

Second, taking it literally does not contradict any other teaching of Scripture. Rather, it complements it in many ways. God instituted marriage (Gen. 2:23-24); God created sex and gave it to humans to enjoy within the bonds of marriage (Gen. 1:27; Prov. 5:17-19); Paul declared that sex should be exercised within a monogamous marriage (1 Cor. 7:1-5); Timothy was informed that sex within marriage should not be forbidden (1 Tim. 4:1-4); and that God "gives us richly all things to enjoy" (1 Tim. 6:17). The Song of Solomon is a beautiful example of a real romance between two actual people that extols the biblical view of sex and marriage. Since a literal marriage does, according to Paul, exemplify the love of Christ for His bride, the church, there is no reason we cannot take this literal love story as a picture of God's love. However, to claim the story is not literally true, or that it is a type or prediction of Christ's love for the church goes beyond the meaning of the text. [The Big Book of Bible Difficulties: Clear and Concise Answers from Genesis to Revelation]

THE *AUTHOR* OF THE BOOK

The Song of Songs, which is Solomon's. Song of Songs 1:1

Ryrie, "Song of Solomon, 1:1 asserts that Solomon wrote this song (among the 1,005 that he wrote, 1 Kings 4:32), although the verse may be translated, "The Song, which is about or concerning Solomon." The contents of the book agree with all that we know about the abilities and wisdom of Solomon, and there is no compelling reason not to regard him as the author."

See 1:1, 5; 3:7,9,11; 8:11-12.

He has authored:

- the book of Proverbs, a book of *Sayings*;
- Ecclesiastes, a book about *Searching*;
- and the Song of Solomon, a book about *Sharing*.

Jewish tradition says that Solomon wrote Proverbs in the prime of his life; Ecclesiastes toward the end of his life; and the Song of Solomon, as a young man.

THE *APPELLATION* OF THE BOOK

The Song of songs - reflecting the first words of the Hebrew text. It is also called the Song of Solomon, because he is the author. And called the Canticles which comes from the Latin. Song of songs is a Hebrew idiom meaning the most exquisite song, the most elegant or beautiful song. The Jewish Midrash calls it "the most praiseworthy, most excellent, most highly treasured among the songs." He wrote many songs but this one was his biggest hit.

shîr is the most common verb in the Old Testament meaning "to sing." It also has the nominal sense of "singer" throughout most of its ninety or so occurrences. The usage of shîr focuses almost exclusively on singing praise to Yahweh. Singing to the Lord as an act of praise for his redemptive deeds is indicated in Exod. 15:1; Judg. 5:1; Isa. 26:1; Jer. 20:13. Singing to the Lord in the specific contexts of worship is recorded in 1 Chr. 16:9; Pss. 13:6; 59:16; 68:4; 96:1 ff. Levitical "singers" are also indicated by the nominal use of shîr (cf. 1 Kgs. 10:12; 1 Chr. 6:33; Ezra 2:41; Neh. 11:22 ff.; 12:28 ff.; Ezek. 40:44). shîr also means "song" in approximately ninety places. Mundane references to "song(s)" include those in Gen. 31:27; 1 Kgs. 4:32; Eccl. 7:5; Isa. 24:9. Songs rendered to Yahweh, praising him for his saving acts of deliverance on behalf of his people, are noted in Exod. 15:1; 2 Sam. 22:1; Isa. 42:10. Songs sung in the context of worship are noted in 1 Chr. 6:31; 2 Chr. 29:27; Pss. 18:1; 67:1; 126:1; Amos 5:23; 8:10. Deut. 31:19 ff. contains the text of a song referred to as the "Song of Moses"—a witness against the people of Israel, to be learned by them as a reminder of their rebellion against Yahweh. shîr is also found in the title of the canonical love poem "Song of Songs" (cf. Song 1:1). [Expository Dictionary of Bible Words: Word Studies for Key English Bible Words Based on the Hebrew and Greek Texts]

THE *APPROXIMATE* DATE

We cannot be absolutely sure, but it seems to have been written sometime during his 40 year reign from 971-931 BC, say 965 BC?

THE *AIM* OF THE LETTER

Historically - it is a romantic love story between King Solomon and a Shulamite woman. It describes their Courtship, Marriage, Consummation, and Continuation after marriage.

"The elder daughter of this poor Shulamite family is a sort of a Cinderella, and she has been forced to keep the vineyard. She is darkened with sunburn from working out in the vineyard. Apparently this family lived in the hill country of Ephraim, and they were tenant farmers. We would call them croppers or hillbillies. We get this picture from a verse in the last chapter (8:11).
I think that is the setting where the first scene takes place. The girl is sunburned and she feels disgraced. In that day a sunburn meant you were a hardworking girl. The women in

the court wanted to keep their skin as fair as they possibly could. It was exactly the opposite of our situation here in California. Here the young girls go down to the beach and lie out in the sun all day in order to get a suntan. Today, it's not a disgrace to have a suntan; in fact, it is a disgrace if you don't have one!

Not only was this girl sunburned from working out in the vineyard, but she says that she was unable to keep her own vineyard. That means she hadn't been to the beauty parlor. Apparently she was a naturally beautiful girl, but she hadn't been able to enhance her beauty or groom herself.

She was an outdoor girl, a hardworking girl. Apparently her brothers also made her watch the sheep (1:8). So she worked in the vineyards and also had to herd the sheep. The place where she worked was along a caravan route there in the hill country. Perhaps some of you have traveled in that land, and you know how rugged it is. A tour bus goes up through there today, and the tourists take a trip into that part of the country. I have been through that rugged territory twice, and I have pictures of some Arab girls working in the fields. I think that is exactly the way it was with the Shulamite girl. When she would look up from her work, she would see the caravans that passed by going

between Jerusalem and Damascus (3:6). She would see the caravans of merchants and also the caravans that carried beautiful ladies of the court. They were the ones who didn't have a sunburn. They had a canopy over them as they traveled on camels or on elephants. The girl would see the beautiful jewels and the satins. She never had anything like that, and she would dream about it, you know.
She also would smell the frankincense and the myrrh as the caravans passed by. One day while the girl was tending her sheep, a handsome shepherd appeared. He fell in love with her. [Thru The Bible with J. Vernon McGee]

Allegorically - Some regard the book purely as an allegory, i.e., fictional characters are employed to teach the truth of God's love for His people. Such a non-historical view, however, is contrary to all principles of normal interpretation and must be rejected.

Illustratively - I believe that while acknowledging it to be historical, we can also see it by way of application, as an illustration of both God's love for Israel and for the Church. This thinking is not foreign to the N.T. (Eph.5:22-33/Rev.21)

Personally - between Christ and the individual believer.

"It portrays the love of Christ for the individual and the soul's communion with Christ...We need to come to the place where it can truly be said of us that we love Him because He first loved us...My friend, may I say that what we need is a personal relationship with Jesus Christ. We need a hot passion for Him. The Lord is not pleased with this cool, lukewarm condition which exists today in the churches among so-called dedicated Christians. Too many who are called dedicated Christians are actually as cold as a cucumber...What we all need is a real, living, burning passion for the person of the Lord Jesus Christ." [Thru The Bible with J. Vernon McGee]

Grasping God's Word, "The Song of Songs is perhaps one of the most shocking books in the Bible because it speaks openly and joyfully of human sexuality. It could be called an R-rated book because of sexually explicit passages. It is in essence a collection of love poems, between a young man and a young woman.

Step 1: What did the text mean to the Biblical audience?

Kinlaw, "The Bible does not see marriage as an inferior state, a concession to human weakness. Nor does it see the normal physical love within that relationship as impure. Marriage was instituted before the Fall, by God, with the command that the first couple become one flesh. Therefore physical love within that conjugal union is good, is God's will, and should be a delight to both partners.

Step 2: Measure the width of the river to the cross. What are the differences between the Biblical audience and us?

We suspect that our wives would not be too flattered if we told them their hair looked like a flock of goats descending from Mount Gilead (4:1) or that their nose resembled the tower of Lebanon looking toward Damascus! (7:4)...We may smile at the idioms and figures used in Song of Songs, but keep in mind that the ancient readers would likewise laugh at translations of our compliments - "She's a babe!" or "He's a hunk!"

AN *ACCEPTABLE* OUTLINE

See Content, at the beginning of this book.

ANOTHER SONG OF LOVE

"Accepting it as a Biblical exegesis that scripture is to be explained by scripture, we believe that the key to the Song of Solomon is Psa. 45, in which the title of that psalm is "A Song of Loves." Psa. 45 is in fact a royal marriage hymn and it refers to Solomon." [J. Sidlow Baxster, Explore the Book]

[1] My heart overflows with a good theme; I address my verses to the King; My tongue is the pen of a ready writer. [2] You are fairer than the sons of men; Grace is poured upon Your lips; Therefore God has blessed You forever. [3] Gird Your sword on *Your* thigh, O Mighty One, *In* Your splendor and Your majesty! [4] And in Your majesty ride on victoriously, For the cause of truth and meekness *and* righteousness; Let Your right hand teach You awesome things. [5] Your arrows are sharp; The peoples fall under You; *Your arrows are* in the heart of the King's enemies. [6] Your throne, O God, is forever and ever; A scepter of uprightness is the scepter of Your kingdom. [7] You have loved righteousness and hated wickedness; Therefore God, Your God, has anointed You With the oil of joy above Your fellows. [8] All Your garments are *fragrant with* myrrh and aloes *and* cassia; Out of ivory palaces stringed instruments have made You

glad. ⁹ Kings' daughters are among Your noble ladies; At Your right hand stands the queen in gold from Ophir. ¹⁰ Listen, O daughter, give attention and incline your ear: Forget your people and your father's house; ¹¹ Then the King will desire your beauty. Because He is your Lord, bow down to Him. ¹² The daughter of Tyre *will come* with a gift; The rich among the people will seek your favor. ¹³ The King's daughter is all glorious within; Her clothing is interwoven with gold. ¹⁴ She will be led to the King in embroidered work; The virgins, her companions who follow her, Will be brought to You. ¹⁵ They will be led forth with gladness and rejoicing; They will enter into the King's palace. ¹⁶ In place of your fathers will be your sons; You shall make them princes in all the earth. ¹⁷ I will cause Your name to be remembered in all generations; Therefore the peoples will give You thanks forever and ever. Psalm 45:1-17

Conclusion

Philips notes, "To turn from Ecclesiastes to the Song of Solomon is like stepping out of the wilderness into the Promised Land. It is like the bright shining of the sun after the rain. God has created human beings with a large number of brain cells devoted to love and sex. This is a fact of our humanity, and it is part of

His design in creation that He declared "good" (Gen. 1:31). But unfortunately, any good thing can be corrupted by ungodly choices. So it is with love and sex.

But these things need not be. Sex - including romance - can be employed for God's glory in accordance with His original design, if the right choices are made. That is what the Song of Songs is about...We must try to appreciate the overall ethical context of the Song of Sons. Monogamous [having only one married partner], heterosexual [a man and a woman] marriage was the proper context for sexual activity, according to God's revelation in the O.T., and God-fearing Israelites would regard the Song in that light. The attitude of the Song itself is the very antithesis of unfaithfulness, either before or after marriage. This is not just love of any kind, but attraction in marriage."

CHAPTER TWO

COURTSHIP

¹For Solomon. The most sublime song of all.

Her (to him): ²Kiss me with the sweet kisses of your lips, for your love delights me more than wine. ³The pleasant aroma of your fragrance rises in the air; your name is like precious perfume poured out: This is why young women adore you. 4Take me away with you; let's run away together! (to the young women) The king has brought me into his bedroom.

Young Women of Jerusalem (to him): We will shout for joy and celebrate over you. We will make it known that your love is better than the finest of wines.

Her (to him): Everyone loves you, and there is no reason why they shouldn't.
[Song of Solomon 1:1-4, The Voice Bible]

"Saturated with stories of sexual escapades, secret rendezvous, and extramarital affairs, today's media teach that immorality means freedom, perversion is natural, and commitment is old-fashioned. Sex, created by

God and pronounced good in Eden, has been twisted, exploited, and turned into an urgent, illicit, casual, and self-gratifying activity. Love has turned into lust, giving into getting, and lasting commitment into "no strings attached." [Life Application Study Bible]

We now are going to begin a study of a Righteous Romance, between Solomon and a Shulamite woman.

THE SHULAMITE'S *DESIRE*

The Shulamite's is thinking of his *Lips*. 1:2a

May he kiss me - "Every kiss is an outward expression of some presumed kind of intimacy. Biblical examples illustrate the wide variety of the nature of that shared intimacy and the degree of mutual commitment involved. Aside from Judas's treacherous kiss, the vast majority of references to kissing are in the OT, and most of these occur in a family context. Kissing as an erotic activity was known and enjoyed in this era, but the image of kissing is primarily between males in the context of a family.
By far the most common biblical examples of kissing involve the warm emotional embracing of relatives or close friends. These are variously indications of intimacy restored

(e.g., Joseph and his brothers, Gen 45:15), the intimacy of reconciliation (Jacob and Esau, Gen 33:4; the prodigal son, Lk 15:20) or intimacy disrupted (Naomi and her daughters-in-law, Ruth 1:9; Paul and the Ephesians elders, Acts 20:37). They also record, in somewhat ritual fashion, occasions of reconciliation, farewell and so forth. All are heavily charged with emotion, as is the extravagant kiss of homage and adoration of the forgiven woman in Luke 7:38. The more formal and conventional "holy kiss" of the early church (Rom 16:16; 1 Cor. 16:20; 2 Cor. 13:12; 1 Thess. 5:26; 1 Pet 5:14) indicates the believers' shared intimacy in the grace of Christ.

The passion of the seductive kiss of illicit lovemaking is well illustrated by the footloose and wayward wife of Proverbs 7:13, who gives hints of the secret pleasures in store for her simpleton victim when she has lured him between the sheets. Appropriate romantic kissing is celebrated in the Song of Songs: "Let him kiss me with the kisses of his mouth" (Song 1:2 NIV).

Of course kissing may represent nothing more than the cynical promises of political campaigning. Absalom's kiss (2 Sam 15:5-6), which stole the hearts of the people of Israel, has its modern counterpart in today's electioneering. Such feigned intimacy may or may not deliver the goods. Judas's kiss (Lk. 22:47), like Joab's sham overture that hoodwinked the unwary Amasa (2 Sam 20:10), was the ultimate in treachery, violating all propriety and social convention. The illicit intimacy with foreign gods is well expressed by Hosea's outraged astonishment, "Men kiss calves!" (Hos. 13:2 RSV). Job also recognized the possibility of secret enticement to worship the astral deities with a kiss of homage (Job 31:26-27). Finally, the metaphorical use of this figure of intimacy (e.g., "righteousness and peace kiss each other," Ps 85:10 NIV) is an indication of how varied are the images of intimacy associated with the idea of kissing." [Dictionary of Biblical Imagery]

with the kisses of - "with the" is a preposition meaning "of, out of, from" and kisses is a plurality, with the repetition of the word "kiss" speaks of intensity. A good translation, "Oh that he would smother me with his kisses." (NEB)

his mouth - "nose kissing" was common in the ancient world, but she was wanting something more intimate. Since we don't do nose kissing today, we could get the meaning - "I don't just want to peck you on the cheek, but to do some serious French kissing!"

Application:

Kiss the Son, lest He be angry, And you perish *in* the way, When His wrath is kindled but a little. Blessed *are* all those who put their trust in Him. Psalm 2:12

My mouth is filled with Your praise And with Your glory all day long. Psalm 71:8

"The kiss indicates the existence of a very personal, close relationship, such as the Lord Jesus with His own. He is able to communicate His message personally to you and me through the Word of God."

Erskine wrote:

His mouth, the joy of heaven, reveals;
His kisses from above
Are pardons, promises, and seals
of everlasting love.

"Those strong desires and earnest longings of the faithful after Christ, flow from a principle of love (Jer. 31:3/Hos.11:4/2 Cor. 5:15/1 Jn.4:10,19). Christ is the ocean of spiritual love, from whence we desire, and into which we return our love: so that our love proceeds from Christ's love." (John Robotham)

Philips, "Some of us have become so accustomed to the great truths of the gospel that they rarely excite us anymore. We have sung since we were children the simple words

Jesus loves me, this I know,
For the Bible tells me so.

Think of the tremendous truth locked up in those simple words! It is an intoxicating truth! It is something better than wine!
"Jesus loves me!" The Son of the living God loves me. He is Creator of the universe, the One whom angels worship. He inhabits eternity, but He has given His heart to me! Paul never ceased to marvel at it. "He loves me!" To think that He loves me, one not worthy to stand for a moment, before Him. Paul described himself as "less than the least of all saints" and as one who deserves the title "chief of sinners." How much more should we realize the wonder of it—He loved me!

Charles H. Gabriel has expressed it thus:

I marvel that He should descend from His throne divine,
To rescue a soul so rebellious and proud as mine;

That He should extend His great love unto such as I,
Sufficient to own, to redeem and to justify!
Oh, it is wonderful that He should care for me enough to die for me!
Oh, it is wonderful, wonderful to me!

His love is tremendously exciting! We should be carving the name of Jesus on every tree! Shouting it from the housetops! Ringing it out as the sweetest music of our souls!

She thinks of his *Love.*

For your love - it is plural indicating (1) the intensity of the love; and (2) the many expressions of love - kissing, hugging, holding hands, even sexual intercourse within the holy bonds of marriage (Prov. 7:18/Song of So. 4:10; 7:12-13/Ezk.16:8; 23:17).

is better than wine - can have the idea of the intoxicating effect that love has on people (Prov. 5:19), or that which gives pleasure and joy (Deut.14:26/Jud.9:13/Psa.4:7; 104:15/Eccles. 2:24-25; 5:18).

Application: Christ is better than wine; better to be intoxicated by Christ, then by wine (Ep.5:18); and He certainly gives greater joy then any we could get from a bottle (1 Pet. 1:8).

Let's prove that Christ's love is better than wine: [Adapted from Spurgeon's sermons, with my own heading]

- Because of what it *Eliminates*.

It is so, first, because it may be taken without question. There may be, and there always will be in the world, questions about wine. There will be some who will say, and wisely say, "Let it alone." There will be others who will exclaim, "Drink of it abundantly;" while a third company will say, "Use it moderately." But there will be no question amongst upright men about partaking to the full of the love of Christ. There will be none of the godly who will say, "Abstain from it;" and none who will say, "Use it moderately;" but all true Christians will echo the words of the Heavenly Bridegroom himself, "Drink, yea, drink abundantly, O beloved." The wisdom of imbibing freely of the love of Christ shall never be questioned even by the pure spirits in heaven; this is the wine which they themselves quaff in everlasting bowls at the right hand of God, and the Lord of glory himself bids them quaff it to their fill. This is the highest delight of all who know Christ, and have been born again by the regenerating power of the Holy Spirit; this is our greatest joy while here below, and we can never have too much of it. Yea, we may even swim in this sea of bliss, and there shall be none who shall dare to ask any one of us, "What do you there?" Many delightful things, many earthly joys, many of the pleasures of this world, are very questionable enjoyments. Christians had better keep away from everything about which their consciences are not perfectly clear; but all our consciences are clear concerning the Lord Jesus, and our heart's love to him; so that, in this respect, his love is better than wine.

- Christ's love is also better than wine, because it is not *Earned.*

Many a man has beggared himself, and squandered his estate, through his love of worldly pleasure, and especially through his fondness for wine; but the love of Christ is to be had without money. What says the Scripture? "Come, buy wine and milk without money and without price." The love of Christ is unpurchased; and I may add that it is unpurchasable. Solomon says, in the eighth chapter of this Book, "If a man would give all the substance of his house for love, it would utterly be contemned," and we may as truly say, "If a man would give all the substance of his house for the love of Christ, it would be utterly contemned." The love of Jesus comes to his people freely; not because they deserve it, or ever will deserve it; not because, by any merits of their own, they have won it, or by any prayers of their own, they have secured it: it is spontaneous love; it flows from the heart of Christ because it must come, like a stream that leaps from an ever-flowing fountain. If you ask why Jesus loves His people, we can give no other reason than this,—"Because it seemed good in his sight." Christ's love is the freest thing in the world,— free as the sunbeam, free as the mountain torrent, free as the air. It comes to the child of God without purchase and without merit, and in this respect it is better than wine.

- Again, Christ's love is better than wine because it is to be enjoyed without worrying about *Excess*.

The sweetest matter on earth, which is for a while pleasant to the taste, sooner or later is too much for the palate. If you find honey, you can soon eat so much of it that you will no longer relish its sweetness; but the love of Jesus never yet is an excess upon the palate of a new-born soul. He who has had most of Christ's love has cried, "More! More! More!" If ever there was a man on earth who had Christ's love in him to the full, it was holy Samuel Rutherford; yet you can see in his letters how he labored for suitable expressions while trying to set forth his hungering and thirsting after the love of Christ. He says he floated upon Christ's love like a ship upon a river, and then he quaintly asks that his vessel may founder, and go to the bottom, till that blessed stream shall flow right over the masthead of his ship. He wanted to be baptized into the love of Christ, to be flung into the ocean of his Savior's love; and this is what the true Christian ever longs for. No lover of the Lord Jesus has ever said that he has had enough of Christ's love. When Madame Guyon had spent many a day and many a month in the sweet enjoyment of the love of Jesus, she penned most delicious hymns concerning it; but they are all full of craving after more, there is no indication that she wished for any change of affection to her Lord, or any change in the object of her affection. She was satisfied with Christ, and longed to have more and more of his love. Ah, poor drunkard! you may put away the cup of devils because you art satiated with its deadly draught; but never did he who drinks of the wine of Christ's love become satiated or even content with it; he ever desires more and yet more of it.

- Christ's love is better than wine, because it is *Excellent.*

All wine has something in it which renders it imperfect, and liable to corruption; there is something that will have to settle, something that must be skimmed off the top, something that needs fining down. So is it with all the joys of earth, there is sure to be something in them that mars their perfection. Men have sought out many inventions of mirth and pleasure, amusement and delight; but they have always found some hitch or flaw somewhere. Solomon gathered to himself all manner of pleasant things that are the delight of kings; he gives us a list of them in the Book of Ecclesiastes: "I made me great works; I built me houses; I planted me vineyards: I made me gardens and orchards, and I planted trees in them of all kind of fruits: I made me pools of water, to water therewith the wood that brings forth trees: I got me servants and maidens, and had servants born in my house; also I had great possessions of great and small cattle above all that were in Jerusalem before me: I gathered me also silver and gold, and the peculiar treasure of rings and of the provinces: I got me men singers and women singers, and the delights of the sons of men, as musical instruments, and that of all sorts;" but his verdict concerning all of them was, "Behold, all was vanity and vexation of spirit."

But he who delights himself in the love of Christ will tell you that he finds no vanity and vexation of spirit there; but everything to charm and rejoice and satisfy the heart. There is nothing in the Lord Jesus Christ that we could wish to have taken away from him; there is nothing in his love that is impure, nothing that is unsatisfactory. Our precious Lord is comparable to the most fine gold; there is no alloy in him; nay, there is nothing that can be compared with him, for "He is altogether lovely," all perfections melted into one perfection, and all beauties combined into one inconceivable beauty. Such is the Lord Jesus, and such is His love to His people without anything of imperfection needing to be removed.

- The love of Christ is better than wine, because it will never *Edulcorate.*

Wine will, turn sour. In certain stages of development, and under certain influences, the sweet ferments, and vinegar is formed instead of wine. Oh, through what fermentations Christ's love might have passed if it had been capable of being acted upon by anything from without! Oh, how often, beloved, have we grieved Him! We have been cold and chill towards Him when we ought to have been like coals of fire. We have loved the things of this world, we have been unfaithful to our Best-beloved, we have suffered our hearts to wander to other lovers; yet never has He been soured toward us, and never will He be. Many waters cannot quench his love, neither can the floods drown it. He is the same loving Savior now as ever He was, and such He always will be, and He will bring us to the rest which remains for the people of God. Truly, in all these respects, because there are none of these imperfections in His love, it is better than wine.

- Christ's love is better than wine, because it produces no ill *Effects.*

Many are the mighty men who have fallen down slain by wine. Solomon says, "Who hath woe? who hath sorrow? who hath contentions? who hath babbling? who hath wounds without cause? who hath redness of eyes? They that tarry long at the wine; they that go to seek mixed wine." But who was ever slain by the love of Christ? Who was ever made wretched by this love? We have been inebriated with it, for the love of Christ sometimes produces a holy exhilaration that makes men say, "Whether in the body, or out of the body, I cannot tell." There is an elevation that lifts the soul above all earthly things, and bears the spirit up beyond where eagles soar, even into the clear atmosphere where God communes with men. There is all that sacred exhilaration about the love of Christ; but there are no evil effects arising from it. He that will, may drink from this golden chalice and he may drink as much as he will, for the more he drinks the stronger and the better shall he be.

Oh, may God grant to us, dear friends, to know the love of Christ, which passes knowledge! I feel sure that, while I am preaching on such a theme as this, I must seem to some here present, to be talking arrant nonsense, for they have never tasted of the love of Jesus; but those who have tasted of it will, perhaps, by my words, have many sweet experiences called to their minds, which will refresh their spirits, and set them longing to have new draughts of this all-precious love which infinitely transcends all the joys of earth. [Spurgeon's Collected Sermons (Met. Tabern. Pul.) - – Metropolitan Tabernacle Pulpit]

Ironside notes, "Wine speaks of anything on earth which stimulates or cheers. When a worldling is cast down and depressed, he says, "Give strong drink to him who is perishing, and wine to those who are bitter of heart. Let him drink and forget his poverty. And remember His misery no more." (Prov.31:6-7). And so wine speaks of the joys of earth to which we once turned before we knew Christ. But after we know Him, we say, "We will remember Your love more than wine...More than wine - one minute spent in fellowship with Him is worth all the joys of earth.

She is pleased with the scent of his *Lotion*

"Your oils have a pleasing fragrance, Your name is like purified oil; Therefore the maidens love you - it was customary in Biblical time to rub the body with fragrant ointments [oil] after a bath in preparation of a festive occasion, or even for a romantic encounter. We would say he used good cologne [Eccles. 7:1; 10:1/Song of Sol. 4:10], making him pleasing and attractive to her; and to women in general. And His Name [person, character, reputation] was as pleasing as his perfume (Mt.12:42). He was identified by His fragrance!

"A person coming into a room wearing perfume attracts immediate attention. It is not necessary for that person to say or do anything. The perfume announces that one's presence. Similarly, the very name of the beloved conjures for the Shulamite a sense of his presence. He did not need to be present physically. His very name brought a quickened beating of her heart and a heightened color to her cheek."

rêaḥ is a noun found in around sixty contexts meaning "smell," or "aroma," in most of these. The "aroma" of sacrifice that is pleasing to God is indicated in Gen. 8:21; Exod. 29:18; Lev. 1:9 ff.; 2:2 ff.; 6:15 ff.; Num. 28:6 ff.; 29:2 ff. The sacrifices of idol worshipers are also "fragrant" incense (i.e., a pleasing aroma) to idols (cf. Ezek. 6:13; 16:19; 20:28). General references to a "fragrant aroma" in relation to perfume are indicated in Song 1:3; 2:12; 4:10. See also Gen. 27:27. [Expository Dictionary of Bible Words]

Ointment - In the Bible the various words associated with perfume can be translated either "ointment" or "perfume." Ointment was a semiviscous liquid or salve that protected one's skin in a harsh climate while imparting a pleasant smell. Its sources were either animals or plants. A Red Sea mollusk was the origin of one perfume used in Palestine. The various plants used to produce perfumes and ointments were brought to Palestine mostly from other lands and included assorted spices, barks, woods, flower petals, seeds, roots, fruits and the resins of certain trees (Gen 37:25; Is 60:6; Jer 6:20). Ointments might also be simple olive oil or the more expensive myrrh or balsam.

Some ointments were extremely rare in the ancient world and costly to obtain and possess. The sage regards ointment as precious (Eccles 7:1). Ointments might be included in the treasury of a king (2 Kings 20:13; Song 3:6-7). The prophet describes the complacent and wealthy of Israel as those who can afford the finest lotions (Amos 6:6). No wonder Jesus' disciples complained at the woman's "waste" of her expensive ointment when she poured it out on Jesus' head. It could have been sold and used more practically to meet the needs of the poor (Mt 26:9; Mk 14:4). In fact, the nard (an ointment probably from Nepal) in Mary's alabaster flask was worth three hundred denarii, nearly a year's wages (Jn 12:5; 11:2; cf. Mk 14:5). Ointment (or oil) is listed among the products that the merchants of the world trade and value (Rev 18:13).

The Bible exhibits several uses of ointment or perfume. The mention of ointment in the apocryphal book of Judith illustrates a common use: after bathing, a woman anointed herself (or her face) with precious ointment, fixed her hair and put on a splendid gown (Jdt 10:3; 16:8; cf. Ruth 3:3; 2 Sam 12:20). Ointment was used as a simple fragrance or cosmetic (Song 1:3; 3:6; 7:13; Mt 6:17). Embalming procedures used ointments, including masking the smell of the dead (2 Chron 16:14; see Burial). After Jesus' hasty execution and burial on Friday, the women spent the next day or so preparing spices and perfumes, expecting to finish their work early on Sunday (Lk 23:56). [Dictionary of Biblical Imagery]

Application:

[14] But thanks be to God, who always leads us in triumph in Christ, and manifests through us the sweet aroma of the knowledge of Him in every place. [15] For we are a fragrance of Christ to God among those who are being saved and among those who are perishing; [16] to the one an aroma from death to death, to the other an aroma from life to life. And who is adequate for these things? 2 Corinthians 2:14-16

Moore notes, "It may be taken to intimate the greater discoveries of the riches of His grace, which have been made to us under the Gospel. Adam had a savor of the ointment in the promise made to him of "the seed of the woman;" Abraham had, as it were, drop of the precious [fragrance] granted to him when rejoicing in the day of Christ, he saw it and was glad. But now, in these Gospel times, the box containing the ointment is broken."

Christ has loved us, and has given Himself for us, an offering and a sacrifice to God for a sweet smelling savor. Unto you therefore which believe He is precious. God also hath highly exalted him, and given him a name which is above every name: that at the name of Jesus every knee should bow. — In Him dwells all the fullness of the Godhead bodily. If you love me, keep my commandments. The love of God is shed abroad in our hearts by the Holy Spirit which is given unto us. The house was filled with the fragrance of the ointment. They took knowledge of them that they had been with Jesus.

O Lord our Lord, how excellent is thy name in all the earth! Who has set Your glory above the heavens. Emmanuel - God with us. His name shall be called Wonderful, Counselor, The Mighty God, The Everlasting Father, and The Prince of Peace. — The name of the Lord is a strong tower: the righteous run into it, and is safe (Ephesians 5:2. 1 Peter 2:7. Philippians 2:9. Colossians 2:9. John 14:15. Romans 5:5. John 12:3. Acts 4:13. Psalm 8:1. Matthew 1:23. Isaiah 9:6. Proverbs 18:10). [Daily Light on the Daily Path]

She *Longs* for him to come to take her away

"Draw me after you and let us run together! The king has brought me into his chambers." "We will rejoice in you and be glad; We will extol your love more than wine. Rightly do they love you." - Better understood as the desires of her heart, "Let the king bring me into his chambers" - rather than a statement of fact." [MacArthur] Her desire is that he would come for her; marry her; and then take her to his bedroom where the marriage would be consummated. This desire would one day be fulfilled (4:1-5:1). The chamber is often a reference to the bedroom (Gen. 43:30/ Jud.15:1; 16:9/2 Sam.13:10/1 Ki.1:15/ Psa.105:30/Isa.26:20).

Application: Our Lord had to draw us to Himself in salvation (Jn. 6:44) and will one day draw us away to meet Him in the air (Jn.14:1-3/1 Thess. 4:16-18). In the meantime the chamber is the secret place of His presence, which we can experience as our Holy of Holies (1 Cor. 6:19/Rev. 3:20).

I am Thine, O Lord, I have heard Thy voice,
And it told Thy love to me;
But I long to rise in the arms of faith
And be closer drawn to Thee.

Refrain

Draw me nearer, nearer blessèd Lord,
To the cross where Thou hast died.
Draw me nearer, nearer, nearer blessèd Lord,
To Thy precious, bleeding side.

Consecrate me now to Thy service, Lord,
By the power of grace divine;
Let my soul look up with a steadfast hope,
And my will be lost in Thine.

Refrain

O the pure delight of a single hour
That before Thy throne I spend,
When I kneel in prayer, and with Thee, my God
I commune as friend with friend!

Refrain

There are depths of love that I cannot know
Till I cross the narrow sea;
There are heights of joy that I may not reach
Till I rest in peace with Thee.

Refrain

Note: The City girls chorus, we have the daughters of Jerusalem to the king. 1:4b
So we have a picture of Romance - involving Lips; Love; Lotion; and Longing...Do we have such intimacy with our Lord?

William Cowper wrote, "Lord, it is my chief complaint, That my love is weak and faint; Yet I love Thee, and adore; O for grace to love Thee more!"

THE SHULAMITES *DESPAIR*

5(to the young women) Look at me, young women of Jerusalem. I am dark but beautiful. I am dark like the tents of Kedar; I am beautiful like the curtains of Solomon's temple. 6Don't stare at my dark skin, for the sun looked down on me. My brothers' anger scorched me; they made me work all day long in the vineyards, So I did not have time to care for my own vineyard, to cultivate my own body. 7(to him) Tell me, my dearest love, where are your sheep grazing today? Where are you resting with your flock at midday? I want to come to you. Why must I go looking for you like the veiled women wandering among the flocks of your friends? Song of Solomon 1:5-7

She is *Black* [outwardly]

I am black - (5:11). This has nothing to do with race. When the bride says here that she is black, she is not referring to her race. She was a Jewish girl from the area of Shunem. She explains the blackness herself. Her family was tenant farmers on one of the vineyards owned by Solomon, and they made her work out in the vineyard. She is sunburned, "I am black, because the sun has looked upon me." She is black, but she is beautiful. Black is beautiful, we hear today. It certainly can be. Black is beautiful when the heart is right with the Lord. The pigment of the skin is of no importance whatever. The condition of the heart is the important matter. Black lives matter – is a good slogan as long as we do not add an *only* to it.

shāḥōr This term is quite rare, occurring only six times as an adjective meaning "black." In Lev. 13:31, 37 it refers to black body hair. Song 1:5 alludes to the dark skin of the Shulamite, and 5:11 to the black hair of her lover. Zech. 6:2, 6 describes black horses. [Expository Dictionary of Bible Words]

The beloved's suntanned appearance revealed that she worked in the fields. This made her feel insecure (do not stare at me) among the city dwellers and in particular the women of Jerusalem. She compared her dark skin to the tents of Kedar, which were made of black goats' hair. The people of Kedar were nomads in northern Arabia who descended from Ishmael (Gen. 25:13). They were known for their archery (Isa. 21:16-17) and flocks (Isa. 60:7; Jer. 49:28-29; Ezek. 27:21; also see Ps. 120:5; Isa. 42:11; Jer. 2:10).

Contrary to the Western idea, that being tanned is a positive thing, in that culture, it was viewed as a negative thing. It reflected a low social status, of one who had to labor in the sun, in contrast to the privileged city girls, who had light skin because they didn't have to work out in it. It would be like a mechanic whose hands stay dirty looking because of his job.

She is *Beautiful* [inwardly]

nā'weh. Beautiful, comely, suitable. Feminine forms are nā'wâ and nāwâ (the latter indistinguishable from nāwâ "pasture"; see no. 1322a). ASV and RSV similar (except Psalm 147:1, see below). This adjective denotes beauty or suitability. Synonyms are tipā'râ "beauty, glory," ṭôb "good, beautiful" (infrequently), ṣebî "decoration, beauty," and

nāʿîm "pleasant, delightful, lovely." Our adjective occurs ten times.
That our adjective can signify beautiful is evident from Song 6:4 where it is parallel to yāpeh. This is especially clear since in this same book our adjective describes one's countenance (Song 2:14, parallel to ʿārēb, pleasant, KB; cf. Song 7:6 [H 7]). The primary female voice retorts that although tanned by the sun and toughened by outside work (Song 1:6), yet she is beautiful (Song 1:5; Jeremiah 6:2). [Theological Wordbook of the Old Testament]

but lovely - two things to note:

- The fact is first *Stated*. 5a

- Then *Illustrated*. 5b

She is Black, "Like the tents of Kedar," they lived in tents make of black goat hair. And she is Beautiful, "Like the curtains of Solomon, referring to the curtains in Solomon's Temple which were beautiful to behold.

Application: "Whenever you enter into the company of the Lord you're in for a shock because you'll be aware of how black you are in and of yourself. You can't be proud and boastful; you can't be self-assured in His presence. His holiness causes us to say, "Woe is me, I am black." Yet we are beautiful, this is because He has cleansed us with His blood; and placed His righteousness upon us. We must always keep the balance - black yet beautiful!" [Courson]

To feel this, and yet also feel one's self in Jesus Christ "lovely as the curtains of Solomon, marks the believer (Ro 7:18; 8:1/2 Cor. 4:7); 1Ti 1:15, "I am chief"; so she says not merely, "I was," but "I am"; still black in herself, but lovely through His loveliness put upon her (Ezk. 16:14).

As one notes, "She is black: here is her natural state-here we have the manifestation of her continued depravity of heart. "I am black, but comely": here is her spiritual condition-the Spirit of God has clothed her with beauteous graces; Christ has washed us and made us fair in His sight. "I am like the tents of Kedar," says she, "the smoke dried curtains of those Arab wanderers who dwelt in this country set forth our sinfulness;" and yet in Christ we can compare ourselves to those embroidered curtains, heavy with gold and silver threads, which hang about the throne of Solomon.

Mankind is not beautiful in the presence of God. Sometimes we tend to think that the reason God is interested in us is because we are such nice, sweet little children. Actually we are ugly; we are sunburned. We are not attractive to Him as we are, but He says that He is going to make us His beautiful bride. That is the wonderful picture given to us in Ephesians 5. The example given to husbands is the love of Christ for the church. "Husbands, love your wives, even as Christ also loved the church, and gave Himself for it; That He might sanctify and cleanse it with the washing of water by the word. That He might present it to Himself a glorious church, not having spot, or wrinkle, or any such thing; but that it should be holy and without blemish" (Eph. 5:25-27). You see, Christ is taking us to the beauty parlor. He will fashion us into His bride, without spot or wrinkle, holy and without blemish! [Thru The Bible with J. Vernon McGee]

She is also *Burned*

By the *Sun*

Do not stare at me because I am swarthy, For the sun has burned me - in Hebrew there is a play on words. Do not look upon me because the sun has looked upon me! Prolonged exposure to the sun made her unusually dark. The sun like the Lord is a great exposure! "The sun's sovereignty is expressed in His unbridled ability to reveal."I am black, because the sun hath looked upon me" (Song of Solomon 1:6). "All things that are reproved are made manifest by the light" (Ephesians 5:13). The dust in the room and the stain on the linen are exposed by sunlight. In like manner the Sun of Righteousness makes bare the brand of our natural birth and the blemishes of our sinful behavior, which disqualify the rich ruler in the Sanhedrin as well as the racial renegade of the Samaritans. "The thing that is hidden brings He forth to light" (Job 28:11).

The most delicate complexion of the highly refined is disregarded by the African sun, and the most cultured soul of sequestered society is exposed as lost and undone under the rays of the Light of the world. "Of a truth I perceive that God is no respecter of persons" (Acts 10:34). The soul that has never recognized its own sordidness knows not the Lord as a Sun."

By her mother's *Son's*

My mother's sons were angry with me; They made me caretaker of the vineyards, But I have not taken care of my own vineyard - Ryrie notes, "My mother's sons. Her stepbrothers made her caretaker of the vineyard, with the result that she could not care for her personal appearance (my own vineyard) as well as other girls could."

My mother's sons were angry with me – Carr observes, "Mention of the role of her brothers, and the omission of any reference to her father anywhere in the song, suggests that the father was dead, and that the brothers were fulfilling the leadership role in the family...No reason is given in the text why the brothers were angry. There is a play on words here, as the root meaning of the verb is "become hot, burn." The similarity between the heat of the sun and the heat of the brothers is evident."

She is *Burdened*

By her *Necessity*

They made me caretaker of the vineyards, But I have not taken care of my own vineyard - The root nāṭar is often used in farming contexts of those who keep or guard vineyards (Song 1:6; Song 8:11-12; cf. Isaiah 5:1-7 for a description of caring for a vineyard). It is also used in the sense of keeping one's anger or wrath. The Lord "keeps wrath for his enemies" (Nahum 1:2), yet he promises not to keep anger forever (Psalm 103:9; Jeremiah 3:5, 12; cf. Amos 1:11). In Leviticus 19:18, a verse which Jesus considered to be at the heart of the OT law (cf. Matthew 19:19; Mark 12:31), Israel is commanded, "You shall not ... bear any grudge (nāṭar) toward the children of your people, but you shall love your neighbor as yourself." [Theological Wordbook of the Old Testament]

Solomon was the owner; her family was responsible for maintaining and producing fruit from the property. But she was the main worker in the family.

By her *Neglect*

But my own vineyard I have not kept - referring to her body.

By her *Need* - to find her lover

⁷ "Tell me, O you whom my soul loves, Where do you pasture your flock, Where do you make it lie down at noon? For why should I be like one who veils herself Beside the flocks of your companions?" ⁸ "If you yourself do not know, Most beautiful among women, Go forth on the trail of the flock And pasture your young goats By the tents of the shepherds.

Where - this is not referring to a specific time, but talking about the hottest time of the day. When do you take a siesta?

Why - why should I be as one who veils herself by the flocks of your companions? It is from the root "wear the veil" or "wrap oneself" so as to hide ones identity. Prostitutes use to veil themselves for fear of being identified by others (Gen. 38:14, Tamar). These prostitutes would come to the flocks during the Siesta to drum up business.

"The girl is saying that she does not want to be mistaken for a prostitute. She is not a loose woman, following the flocks looking for any lover. She has made a commitment to one. And she wants to know where she can find him." [Expositor's Bible Commentary]

Application: We are those who seek the Lord and Him alone. We are not after many lovers - just one. We don't keep our own vineyard we are not self-centered and self-absorbed but are always seeking more intimacy with Him.

Spurgeon, "She expresses her longing to be with Him. The desire of a renewed soul is to find Christ, and spend time with Him. And to do this takes self-depreciation. Why is it that the best Christians depreciate themselves the most? Is it not because they are most accustomed to looking within? In his anxiety to be pure from evil, the godly man will be eager to notice and quick to detect, the least particle of defilement."

Can ye cleave to your Lord?
Can ye cleave to your Lord,
When the many turn aside?
Can ye witness he hath the living Word,
And none upon earth beside?
And can ye endure with the Virgin band,
The lowly and pure in heart,
Who, whithersoever their Lamb doth lead,
From his footsteps ne'er depart?
Do ye answer, 'We can?' Do ye answer, 'We can,
Through his love's constraining power?'
But ah remember the flesh is weak,
And will shrink in the trial-hour?
Yet yield to his love, who round you now,
The bands of a man would cast;
The cords of his love, who was given for you,
To the altar binding you fast."

THE SHULAMITE IS *DESCRIBED*

Him (to her): [8]If you do not know where I am, most beautiful of women, Follow the tracks of my sheep— they will lead you to me— And graze your flocks of young goats beside the shepherds' tents. ⁹You remind me, my dear, of an honored mare among Pharaoh's stallion-driven chariots; ¹⁰The strings of jewels against your cheeks frame your elegance, as also the tender curve of your neck with precious gems.

Young Women of Jerusalem (to her): ¹¹We will make for you golden jewelry to lay against your skin, golden jewelry studded with silver to frame your elegance.

Her: ¹²When the king was relaxing at his table, the seductive fragrance of my perfume filled the air. ¹³My love is close to my heart, like a sachet of myrrh tucked between my breasts. ¹⁴My love is like a fragrant bouquet of henna blossoms from the vineyards of Engedi.

Him: 15How beautiful you are, my dear! How so very beautiful! Your eyes are like doves.

Her: 16You, my love, are so handsome! A pleasure to behold! Our bed is a lush, green field, 17The beams of our house are majestic cedars, and the rafters are tall pines.

Her: 1I am a rose of Sharon, a lily found in one of the valleys. **Him**: 2Like a lily among thorns, that is what she is; my dear is a captivating beauty among the young women.

Her: 3My love is like an apple tree in a wooded forest; he is a ripe tree among a grove of saplings, those young men. I sat beneath his ample shade, filled with such joy. I tasted the sweetness of his fruit and longed for more. 4He placed me at his banquet table, for everyone to see that his banner over me declares his love. 5(to those around) Sustain me with sweet raisins. Refresh my energy with apples Because I am lovesick for him. 6His left hand cradles my head; his right embraces me. 7(to the young women) You of Jerusalem heed my warning. By the gazelles and deer of the field, I charge you not to excite your love until it is ready. Don't stir a fire in your heart too soon, until it is ready to be satisfied. 8I hear his voice! The voice of my love! Here he comes, Leaping over the mountains, bounding among the hills. 9My love is like a gazelle, sure-footed and swift as a young stag. Look, there he is! Standing behind my wall, watching through the windows, peering through the lattice. 10My love responded and said to me,

Him: Arise, my dearest, my beauty, and come away with me. 11Don't you see? The winter is done. The rains and clouds have come and gone. 12The flowers are unfolding in the fields; the birds are warming up their songs, The cooing of the turtledove is heard throughout the land. 13The fig trees are bringing forth their first fruit, and the vines are in blossom, filling the air with their fragrance. So arise my dearest, my beauty, and come away with me. 14Now, my dove, don't be shy. Don't hide from me in the clefts of the rock or nest like a bird in secret among the cliffs. Show me your lovely form. Let me hear your beautiful voice, For it sounds so sweet, and your face is so lovely.

Young Women of Jerusalem (to the couple): 15Catch the foxes for us, those little foxes that menace the vineyards, For our vineyards are so vulnerable when they are in full bloom.

Her: 16My love is mine, and I am his. He grazes among my lilies. 17As the day breathes its morning breeze and shadows turn and flee, Turn to me, my love, like a gazelle; come to me like a young stag on rugged mountains.

Her: ^{1}Restless night after night in my bed, I longed and looked for my soul's true love; I searched for him, but I could not find him. $_2$I will get up now and search the city, wander up and down streets and plazas; I will look for my soul's true love. I searched for him, but I could not find him. ^{3}The watchmen found me as they kept watch on the silent city. "Have you seen my soul's true love?" I asked. ^{4}Not long after I left them, I found him— I found my soul's true love. I pulled him to me and would not let him go until I brought him to my mother's house, to the very room where she conceived me. ^{5}(to the young women of Jerusalem) Heed my warning: By the gazelles and deer of the field, I charge you not to excite your love until it is ready. Don't stir a

fire in your heart too soon, until it is ready to be satisfied.
Young Women of Jerusalem: ^{6}Who is this coming up from the desert, with billowing clouds of dust and smoke, with a sweet aroma of burning myrrh and frankincense, with fragrant spices fresh from the merchant? ^{7}Look, it is Solomon's litter, surrounded by 60 strong men, some of the very best soldiers in Israel, ^{8}All armed swordsmen, battle-hardened heroes, experts at war, Marching with swords at their sides, ready to guard the king from the terrors of the night. ^{9}King Solomon built his own royal carriage from the trees of Lebanon. ^{10}He had its posts fashioned from silver, its back made of gold, its seat covered with royal purple, its interior decorated with love by the young women of Jerusalem. ^{11}O go out, young women of Zion, and see King Solomon Wearing the crown with which his mother has crowned him on his wedding day, on the day his heart overflows with joy. [The Voice Bible: Step Into the Story of Scripture (p. 785). Thomas Nelson. Kindle Edition]

Charles Stanley, "Love is the greatest gift God offers us, and yet it is the one we have the most difficulty receiving. Why? First, we do not think we deserve His love - which is true (Rom. 5:8). Second, we do not understand it, for the quality of His love differs tremendously from our own. We somehow want to believe that He loves us the way we love others. Such a viewpoint, however, leaves us doubtful that He will always love us as the Bible promises He will. We must remember that God's love is not based on emotion, but flows out of His changeless character (1 Jn.4:8). Since it is impossible for Him to do anything contrary to His nature, His love will forever remain certain and dependable. Every day you and I walk under the canopy of God's amazing love, which remains perfect and changeless, even if we wander from His will or fall into disobedience. God has always loved you and always will."

The Song of Solomon is not only a love story between Solomon and a Shulamite woman, but also illustrates a love story between God and His people. The Shulamite is Described (Song of Solomon 1:8-3:5).

She is the *Fairest*

If you yourself do not know, most beautiful among women... [15] *How beautiful you are, my darling, How beautiful you are!* - Solomon refuses her negative evaluation of herself. To him she is beautiful! 1:8, 15-16; 2:10,13; 4:1,7; 5:9; 6:1,4,10. Fairest refers to physical beauty (Gen. 12:11, 14; 29:17). Occurring about forty times in the Hebrew Bible, this adjective is only attested elsewhere in Semitic in a Tell el-Amarna gloss and in Middle Hebrew. It refers exclusively to physical beauty. The object modified by this adjective can be anything which exists in the earthly realm. Both individual males (e.g., David; 1 Sam. 16:12) and females (e.g., Tamar, Absalom's half sister; 2 Sam. 13:1) are described by this adjective, as are collectives (women; Prov. 11:22). It is also used to describe other living entities, such as cows (Gen. 41:2) and trees (Jer. 11:16). Yāpheh is used metaphorically in Prov. 11:22: "Like a gold ring in a swine's snout is a beautiful woman without discretion." Beauty as an ideal describes Zion (Ps. 48:2). Never is it used for Yahweh. [Complete Biblical Library] While it is proper and Biblical to acknowledge our unworthiness, the Lord views us as beautiful in Christ (Rom. 8:30/ Eph.5:25-27).

Spurgeon, "I would rather trust Christ's eyes than mine. If my eyes tell me I am black I will weep but if He assures me I am fair I will believe Him and rejoice. Some saints are more apt to remember their sinfulness and grieve over it than to believe in their righteousness in Christ and triumph in it. The Lord Jesus, after He had washed His disciples feet, said, "He who is bathed needs only to wash his feet, but is completely clean; and you are clean"

(Jn.13:10), that is why Paul declared "Who can bring a charge against God's elect" no one, not even us!"

She is to *Follow*

Go forth on the trail of the flock And pasture your young goats By the tents of the shepherds - she is instructed to follow the foot prints left by his sheep.

This is commanded over and over again, that we are to seek our Lord, always with the promise that we will find Him (Deuteronomy 4:7 Psalm 16:8 Psalm 35:22 Psalm 38:21 Psalm 71:12 Psalm 75:1 Psalm 119:151 Psalm 145:18 Isaiah 50:8 Isaiah 55:6 Jeremiah 23:23 Lamentations 3:57 Matthew 20:30 Acts 2:25 Acts 17:27 Romans 10:6 Revelation 3:20).

- *Whom* to seek -"Seek ye the Lord" (Isa. 55:6).
- *When* to seek - "First" (Matt. 6:33); "Early" (Psa. 63:1); "Continually" (1 Chron. 16:11).
- *What* to seek - "Peace" (Psa. 34:14); God's "Precepts" (Psa. 119:45); "Good" (Amos 5:14); "Righteousness and Meekness" (Zeph. 2:3); "Things above" (Col. 3:1).

- *How* to seek -with a "prepared heart" (2 Chron 19:3; 30:19); with a prayerful spirit (Dan. 9:3; Matt. 7:7).
- *Why* we should seek - because we "shall not want" (Psa. 34:10). [Handbook of Bible Application]

Someday, watch a stream of ants stretching between their anthill and a food source. Some will be going to pick up their load; others will be returning to deposit their prize in the recesses of the anthill. The whole process will be very organized, very precise. Then ask yourself, "Why are these ants so organized in their task?" The reason is that ants are good followers, each dependent on the ant in front of him to lead him to the food supply. Because each ant follows the other, there is a straight line between the anthill and the food—no wasted energy, no unnecessary detours. There is a lesson in that for would-be disciples. The One who is Head Leader, whom we all follow, is Christ. (1 Cor. 11:1).

She is like a *Filly*

To me, my darling, you are like My mare among the chariots of Pharaoh - Solomon knew horses, of which he brought from Egypt, a place famous for their horses (1 Ki. 10:26-29). Chariots were pulled by stallions not fillies [which is a young female horse]. As a result, a filly in heat was used as a defensive method. As the chariots drew near, a filly in heat would be let lose nearby, this would cause the stallions to be distracted from their intended targets. His point is that she drives all men crazy with her attractiveness, as well as Solomon himself. Of course comparing her to a horse, in that day, also spoke of beauty and strength.

Kinlaw, "We have forgotten what a thing of beauty a horse can be when compared to other animals. We are also unaware what valuable creatures they were in that ancient world. They were beautiful in themselves."

"In comparing the beauty of the Shulamite to a "filly," Solomon was being very gracious, because the horse in the Orient was a cherished companion and not a beast of burden. Solomon was praising his bride for her beauty and graceful movements. In addition, stallions and not fillies or mares would pull a chariot of Pharaoh..." [Baptist Study Bible]

She is naturally beautiful, without the need of being decked in *Fine* Jewelry. 10-11

[10] *"Your cheeks are lovely with ornaments, Your neck with strings of beads."* [11] *"We will make for you ornaments of gold With beads of silver."* - kelî is a term with a somewhat

generalized semantic range throughout most of its three hundred occurrences. The word conveys the general idea of a utensil, implement, or tool. It also refers to nondescript items such as "things." However, on about twenty occasions, kelî refers to jewelry or jewels. There are a number of texts in which kelî refers to precious metals such as gold or silver (cf. Gen. 24:53; Exod. 35:22; Num. 31:50 ff.; Ezek. 16:17, 39). In particular, Exod. 3:22, 11:2, 12:35 refer to the precious stones taken as "plunder" from the Egyptians when the Israelites escaped from their enslavement in Egypt. Jewelry is mentioned in a non-specific sense in 2 Chr. 20:25; Prov. 20:15; Song 1:10; Isa. 61:10; Ezek. 23:26.

Horses were decked in fine jewelry. Either she decked out with such jewelry or more likely this is describing what he wants to do for her. This reminds us of what the Lord wants to do for us…The king moves from considering the decorations on the mare to the ornaments on his lover. Having been a poor country girl, she is not only conscious of her sun-tanned skin but also of her lack of jewelry. But the king will rectify this. Out of his great wealth he will adorn her with jewelry fit for such a bride. Likewise Christ, the rich bridegroom of heaven, will adorn his bride the church with the jewels of grace and truth. He is even now preparing her for the great marriage supper of the Lamb. [New Bible Commentary: 21st century edition]

Her *Fragrance* is pleasing. 12-14

[12] "While the king was at his table, My perfume gave forth its fragrance. [13] "My beloved is to me a pouch of myrrh Which lies all night between my breasts. [14] "My beloved is to me a cluster of henna blossoms In the vineyards of Engedi." - her fragrance is noticeable and pleasing to him.

"First Kings 4 says that at Solomon's table every day there were 30 measures [190 bushels] of fine flour, threescore measures [390 bushels] of meal, 10 fat oxen, 20 oxen out of pasture, 100 sheep besides harts, roe-bucks, fallow deer, and fatted fowl. Solomon's table was abundant in provision. We likewise feats on the Lord's bounty (Eph.1:3). A bundle of myrrh is my beloved to me, that lies all night between my breasts - Myrrh is a fragrance made from the bark of a tree found in Arabia and India, and was traditionally used for embalming the dead, as well as, to make a person sweet-smelling. Henna was a Palestinian shrub. It was used to color hair, finger nails, etc. Its blossoms were quite fragrant, which is what is being referred to here.

12 When my King-Lover lay down beside me, my fragrance filled the room. 13 His head resting between my breasts— the head of my lover was a sachet of sweet myrrh. 14 My beloved is a bouquet of wildflowers picked just for me from the fields of Engedi. Song of Songs 1:12-14 (MSG)

shad. Breast, bosom. This noun occurs twenty-one times, twenty-four if one adds the three appearances of shōd in Job 24:9; Isaiah 60:16; Isaiah 66:11). Eight of these are found in the Song of Solomon. Four of these are located in the intimate description by the groom of his bride: Song 4:5; Song 7:3, 7, 8 [H 4, 8, 9]. Once the bride refers to her own breasts as a resting place for her lover's head (Song 1:13). There are two references to the undeveloped breasts of the "little sister" (?) (Song 8:8, 10) and one to the mother of the bride (Song 8:1). It should not be perplexing that in the OT canon there is at least one book devoted to the portrayal, among other things, of the physical side of the marriage relationship, the function of which is so clearly spelled out in Genesis 1-2.
Besides the Song of Solomon passages the Hebrew word shad is used in the following

contexts: (1) in a decidedly erotic, sensual situation where adultery and seduction are prominent: Hosea 2:2 [H 4]; Ezekiel 23:3, 21 where shad is parallel with dad "the (nipple of the) breast"; (2) as a gesture of mourning, Isaiah 32:12; Ezekiel 23:34 (cf. "he smote upon his breast -stēthos," Luke 18:13 and also Luke 23:48); (3) as an indication of arrival at maturity and young adulthood and hence responsible for one's conduct or able to receive instruction: Ezekiel 16:7; Isaiah 28:9 (off the bottle!); (4) as a blessing of fertility and progeny, Genesis 49:25, or the withholding of the same in judgment, Hosea 9:14. In those days when bottle feeding of babies was unknown, dry breasts could be a tragedy indeed. [Theological Wordbook of the Old Testament]

Spurgeon, "Jesus Christ is like myrrh. Myrrh may be well the type of Christ for its preciousness. It was an exceedingly expensive drug. We know that Jacob sent some of it down into Egypt as being one of the choice products of the land. It is always spoken of in Scripture as being a rich, rare, and costly substance. But no myrrh could ever compare with Him, for Jesus Christ is so precious, that if heaven and earth were put together they could not buy another Savior. When God gave to the world his Son, He gave the best that heaven had. Take Christ out of heaven, and there is nothing for God to give. Christ was God's all, for is it not written, "In him dwelleth all the fullness of the Godhead bodily?" Oh! precious gift of the whole of deity in the person of Christ! How inestimably precious is that body of his which he took of the substance of the virgin! Well might angels herald the coming of this immaculate Savior, well might they watch over His holy life, for He is precious in his birth, and precious in all His actions. How precious is He, dear friends, as myrrh in the offering of His great atonement! What a costly sacrifice was that! At what a price were ye redeemed! Not with silver and gold, but with the precious blood of Christ. How precious is He too, in His resurrection! He justifies all His people at one stroke-rising from the dead-that glorious sun scatters all the nights of all His people by one rising. How precious is He in his ascension, as He leads captivity captive, and scattereth gifts among men! And how precious to-day in those incessant pleadings of His through which the mercies of God come down like the angels upon Jacob's ladder to our needy souls! Yes, He is to the believer in every aspect like myrrh for rarity and excellence.

Myrrh, again, was pleasant. It was a pleasant thing to be in chamber perfumed with myrrh. Through the nostrils myrrh conveys delight to the human mind; but Christ gives delight to His people, not through one channel, but through every avenue. It is true that all His garments smell of myrrh, and aloes, and cassia, but He has not spiritual smell alone, the taste shall be gratified too, for we eat His flesh and drink His blood. Nay, our feeling is ravished, when His left hand is under us and His right hand doth embrace us. As for His voice it is most sweet, and our soul's ear is charmed with its melody. Let God give Him to our sight, and what can our eyes want more? Yea, He is altogether lovely. Thus every gate of the soul has commerce with Christ Jesus in the richest and rarest commodities. There is no way by which a human spirit can have communion with Jesus which does not yield unto that spirit fresh and varied delights. O beloved, we cannot compare Him merely to myrrh. He is everything which is good to look upon, or to taste, or to handle, or to smell-all put together in one, the quintessence of all delights. As all the rivers run into the sea, so all delights center into Christ. The sea is not full, but Jesus is full to the very brim. Moreover, myrrh is perfuming. It is used to give a sweet smell to other things. It was mingled with the sacrifice, so that it was not only the smoke of the fat of kidneys of rams, and the flesh of fat beasts, but there was a sweet fragrance of myrrh, which went up with

the sacrifice to heaven. And surely, beloved, Jesus Christ is very perfuming to His people. Does not He perfume their prayers, so that the Lord smelleth a sweet savor? Does He not perfume their songs, so that they become like vials full of odour sweet? Does He not perfume our ministry, for is it not written, "He causeth us to triumph in Christ, and maketh manifest the savor of His knowledge by us in every place. For we are unto God a sweet savor of Christ, in them that are saved, and in them that perish." Our persons are perfumed with Christ. Whence get we our spikenard but from Him? Whither shall we go to gather camphire which shall make our persons and presence acceptable before God but to Him? "For we are accepted in the beloved." "Ye are complete in him"- "perfect in Christ Jesus"- "for He has made us kings and priests unto our God, and we shall reign for ever and ever."
Myrrh has preserving qualities. The Egyptians used it in embalming the dead: and we find Nicodemus and the holy women bringing myrrh and aloes in which to wrap the dead body of the Savior. It was used to prevent corruption. What is there which can preserve the soul but Christ Jesus?"

Her *Facial Features* are attractive

"How beautiful you are, my darling, How beautiful you are! Your eyes are like doves." -

"In the ancient Near East there was unusual emphasis on the beauty of a woman eyes. This was probably due to the practice of women veiling themselves and wearing long robes so that no portion of her body or face was exposed except for their eyes. The only indication of a woman's beauty was her eyes." The eyes were regarded as a source of beauty (1 Sam 16:12; Song 1:15; 4:1, 9; 5:12; 6:5; 7:4).

eyes like doves - In their wild state doves generally build their nests in the clefts of rocks, but when domesticated "dove-cots" are prepared for them (Song 2:14; Jer. 48:28; Isa 60:8). The dove was placed on the standards of the Assyrians and Babylonians in honor, it is supposed, of Semiramis (Jer. 25:38); Vulg., "fierceness of the dove;" comp. (Jer. 46:16; Jer. 50:16). Doves and turtle-doves were the only birds that could be offered in sacrifice, as they were clean according to the Mosaic law (Gen 15:9; Lev 5:7; Lev 12:6; Luke 2:24). The dove was the harbinger of peace to Noah (Gen 8:8, 10). It is often mentioned as the emblem of purity (Ps 68:13). It is a symbol of the Holy Spirit (Gen 1:2; Mat 3:16; Mark 1:10; Luke 3:22; John 1:32); also of tender and devoted affection (Song 1:15; Song 2:14). David in his distress wished that he had the wings of a dove that he might fly away and be at rest (Ps 55:6-8). There is a species of dove found at Damascus "whose feathers, all except the wings, are literally as yellow as gold" (Ps 68:13). [Illustrated Bible Dictionary]

The suggestions are many:

- Arabic love literature describes doves having sentimental eyes.
- The comparison is said to be related to the color of her eyes.
- Others related it to the quick movement of the doves eyes, indicating the lively motion of her eyes.
- One notes that it had to do with the fluttering of her eyes, which reminded him of the fluttering of a doves wings.
- Many attribute it to softness.

"This, surely, is what the Lord Jesus desires to see in us. He desires to see all of the glories and graces of His Holy Spirit. Are our eyes round with wonder as we gaze upon Him? Does His heart come to rest when He thinks of us just as Noah's dove found rest, not in a dead world but in Noah's hand? He brings peace to us; do we bring peace to Him? It was not a raven that the beloved saw in the Shulamite, nor an eagle or a hawk, but a dove. Is that what Christ sees in us?"

Their meeting place is likened to a beautiful *Forest*. 16-17

¹⁶ "How handsome you are, my beloved, And so pleasant! Indeed, our couch is luxuriant! ¹⁷ "The beams of our houses are cedars, Our rafters, cypresses - "סרע eres, from its use in several places of the Hebrew Bible, generally signifies a mattress; and here probably a green bank is meant, on which they sat down, being now on a walk in the country. Or it may mean a bower in a garden, or the nuptial bed." [A Commentary and Critical Notes]

"They have made their bed out in the country. The adjective that qualified the bed is an interesting one. It means flourishing, green, luxurious. This Hebrew adjective is more appropriate to a tree, but that is the point. We are dealing with figurative language here. We are not to interpret this as an actual event. The woman describes the "house," where she will share a moment of intimacy with her lover. The picture is of a well-forested area where there is a grassy opening. They are surrounded - that is, protected - by trees. The trees provided privacy, and more, the cedar and the juniper are trees produce a pleasant scent, making this spot a pleasant place for an intimate encounter." [Longman]

The Bridegroom is beautiful to those of us who believe. He is altogether lovely. Augustine wrote: "He is fair in heaven, fair in the earth; fair in the virgin's womb [He was that holy thing], fair in the arms of His parents, fair in the miracles, fair in His stripes... fair in laying down His life, fair in receiving it again; fair on the cross, fair in the sepulcher." This was the way Augustine, that great saint of God of the past, described the Lord Jesus.

From every point our Well-beloved is most fair. Our various experiences are meant by our heavenly Father to furnish fresh standpoints from which we may view the loveliness of Jesus; how amiable are our trials when they carry us aloft where we may gain clearer views of Jesus than ordinary life could afford us! We have seen Him from the top of Amana, from the top of Shenir and Hermon, and He has shone upon us as the sun in his strength; but we have seen Him also "from the lions' dens, from the mountains of the leopards," and He has lost none of His loveliness. From the languishing of a sick bed, from the borders of the grave, have we turned our eyes to our soul's spouse, and He has never been otherwise than "all fair." Many of His saints have looked upon Him from the gloom of dungeons, and from the red flames of the stake, yet have they never uttered an ill word of Him, but have died extolling His surpassing charms. Oh, noble and pleasant employment to be forever gazing at our sweet Lord Jesus! Is it not unspeakably delightful to view the Savior in all His offices, and to perceive Him matchless in each?—to shift the kaleidoscope, as it were, and to find fresh combinations of peerless graces? In the manger and in eternity, on the cross and on His throne, in the garden and in His kingdom, among thieves or in the midst of cherubim, He is everywhere "altogether lovely." Examine carefully every little act of His life, and every trait of His character, and He is as lovely in the minute as in the majestic. Judge Him as you will, you cannot censure; weigh Him as you please, and He will not be found wanting. Eternity shall not discover the shadow of a spot in our Beloved, but rather, as ages revolve, His hidden glories shall shine forth with yet more inconceivable splendor, and His unutterable loveliness shall more and more ravish all celestial minds. [Morning and Evening]

She sees herself as a common *Flower*

[1] "I am the rose of Sharon, The lily of the valleys." [2] "Like a lily among the thorns, So is my darling among the maidens."

THE BELOVED TO HER LOVER: 1 I am a meadow flower from Sharon, a lily from the valleys. THE LOVER TO HER BELOVED: 2 Like a lily among the thorns, so is my darling among the maidens. Song of Songs 2:1-2 (NET1)

Her *Comparison*

I am the rose of Sharon. And the lily of the valleys – this is a very known verse from this book, but often misapplied.

Wiersbe, "She compares herself to a common crocus (rose) from Sharon and an ordinary hyacinth (lily) of the fields (2:1). In spite of what a familiar Gospel song says, it is the Shulamite who makes this comparison of herself and not the king who make this comparison of himself.' [Bible Exposition Commentary - Old Testament - The Bible Exposition Commentary – Wisdom and Poetry]

"Here the beloved spoke of herself as a rose of Sharon, the fertile coastal region of Israel from Caesarea to Joppa. The Hebrew word for rose is ḥăbaṣṣelet. In Isaiah 35:1, its only other occurrence in the Old Testament, it is translated "crocus," which may be the meaning here. It was a common meadow flower. The lily too was a common flower mentioned often in the Song of Songs (2:1-2, 16; 4:5; 5:13; 6:2-3; 7:2). Though in her humility she likened herself to common flowers of the field..." [The Bible Knowledge Commentary: An Exposition of the Scriptures by Dallas Seminary Faculty]

rose -- if applied to Jesus Christ, it, with the white lily (lowly, 2Co 8:9), answers to "white and ruddy" (Song 5:10). But it is rather the meadow-saffron: the Hebrew means radically a plant with a pungent bulb, inapplicable to the rose. So Syriac. It is of a white and violet color [MAURER, GESENIUS, and WEISS]. The bride thus speaks of herself as lowly though lovely, in contrast with the lordly "apple" or citron tree, the bridegroom (Song 2:3); so the "lily" is applied to her (Song 2:2), Sharon -- (Isa 35:1, 2). In North Palestine, between Mount Tabor and Lake Tiberias (1Ch 5:16)." [A Commentary: Critical, Experimental, and Practical on the Old and New Testaments]

Heb "meadow-saffron" or "crocus." The noun חֲבַצֶּלֶת (khavatselet) traditionally has been translated "rose" (KJV, NKJV, ASV, NASB, RSV, NRSV, NIV, NJPS, NLT, CEV); however, recent translations suggest "crocus" (NIV margin, NJPS margin), "narcissus" (DBY) or simply "flower" (DRA, NAB). The LXX translated it with the generic term ἄνθος (anthos, "flower, blossom"). Early English translators knew that it referred to some kind of flower but were unsure exactly which type, so they arbitrarily chose "rose" because it was a well-known and beautiful flower. In the light of comparative Semitics, modern Hebrew lexicographers have settled on "asphodel," "meadow-saffron," "narcissus," or "crocus" The Hebrew term is related to Syriac hamsalaita ("meadow saffron") and Akkadian habasillatu ("flower-stalk, marsh plant, reed"). Lexicographers and botanists suggest that the Hebrew term refers to Ashodelos (lily family), Narcissus tazetta (narcissus or daffodil), or Colchicum autumnale (meadow-saffron or crocus). The location of this flower in Sharon suggests that a common wild flower would be more consonant than a rose. The term appears elsewhere only in Isa 35:1 where it refers to some kind of desert flower - erroneously translated "rose" (KJV, NJPS) but probably "crocus" (NASB, NIV, NJPS margin). Appropriately, the rustic maiden who grew up in the simplicity of rural life compares herself to a simple, common flower of the field (M. H. Pope, Song of Songs [AB], 367). [NET Bible]

His *Compliment*

Like a lily among thorns, so is my love among

the maidens - The Lover accommodates her self-denigrating comparison, but heightens it to praise her: If she insisted that she was nothing more than a common flower of the field, then he insisted that all other women were like thorns by comparison. The term חוֹח (khokh, "thorn") is often used as a figure for utter desolation and the cause of pain; it is the antithesis of fertility and beautiful luxuriant growth (Job 31:40; Isa 34:13; Hos 9:6). [NET Bible]

Reminds me of the common bush found out in the desert, it was nothing until the fire of God descended upon it. Then God's beauty shone through it. See my book *Spiritual Survivor Man*.

"Yet once more I think many a child of God may regard himself as still being a lily among thorns, because of his afflictions. Certainly the church is so, and she is thereby kept for Christ's own. If thorns made it hard for Him to reach us for our salvation, there is another kind of thorn which makes it hard for any enemy to come at us for our hurt. Our trials and tribulations, which we would fain escape from, often act as a spiritual protection: they hedge us about and ward off many a devouring foe. Sharp as they are, they serve as a fence and a defense. Many a time, dear child of God, you would have been an exposed lily, to be plucked by any ruthless hand, if it had not been that God had placed you in such circumstances that you were shut up unto Himself. Sick saints and poor saints and persecuted saints are fair lilies enclosed by their pains, and wants, and bonds that they may be for Christ alone. I look on John Bunyan in prison writing his "Pilgrim's Progress," and I cannot help feeling that it was a great blessing for us all that such a lily was shut up among the thorns that it might shed its fragrance in that famous book, and thereby perfume the church for ages. You that are kept from roaming by sickness or by family trials need not regret these things, for perhaps they are the means of making you more completely your Lord's. How charmingly Madame Guyon wrote when she was immured in a dungeon. Her wing was closely bound, but her song was full of liberty, for she felt that the bolts and bars only shut her in -with her Beloved, and what is that but liberty? She sang

"A little bird I am,
Shut from the fields of air;
And in my cage I sit and sing
To him who placed me there;
Well pleased a prisoner to be,
Because, my God, it pleaseth thee.

"Nought have I else to do,
I sing the whole day long;
And He whom most I love to please
Doth listen to my song;
He caught and bound my wandering wing;
But still he bends to hear me sing."

"As the lily among thorns," she lived in prison shut in with her Lord, and since the world was quite shut out, she was in that respect a gainer. O to have one's heart made as "a garden enclosed, a spring shut up, a fountain sealed." So let my soul be, ay, so let it be even if the enclosure can only be accomplished by a dense growth of trials and griefs. May every pain that comes and casts us on our bed, and lays us aside from public usefulness; may every sorrow which arises out of our business, and weans us from the world; may every adversary that assails us with bitter, taunting words only thicken the thorn hedge which encases us from all the world, and constrains us to be chaste lilies set apart for the Well-beloved. [Spurgeon's Collected Sermons [Metropolitan Tabernacle Pulpit]

She views him as a *Fruit* tree

Like an apple tree among the trees of the forest, So is my beloved among the young men. In his shade I took great delight and sat down, And his fruit was sweet to my taste.

He is compared to an apple tree in a forest, which in that day would be considered a valuable and unusual find. In all the above references the true apple, Pyrus malus, suits the conditions satisfactorily. The apple tree affords good shade, the fruit is sweet, the perfume is a very special favorite with the people of the East. Sick persons in Palestine delight to hold an apple in their hands, simply for the smell. (Compare Arabian Nights, "Prince Hassan and the Paribanou.") Further, the Arabic for apple, tuffah, is without doubt identical with the Hebrew tappūaḥ. The apple was well known, too, in ancient times; it was, for example, extensively cultivated by the Romans. The one serious objection is that apples do not easily reach perfection in Palestine; the climate is too dry and hot; farther north in the Lebanon they flourish. At the same time it is possible to exaggerate this objection, for with careful grafting and cultivation exceedingly good apples may be produced in the mountain regions. Apple trees there need special care and renewal of the grafts, but there is no impossibility that at the time of the writing of Canticles skilled gardeners should have been able to produce sweet and perfumed apples in Palestine. Small but very sweet and fragrant apples are now grown at Gaza. Good apples are now plentiful in the market at Jerusalem, but they are chiefly importations from the North. [The International Standard Bible Encyclopedia]

The aesthetic qualities of trees are occasionally mentioned in the Bible. Genesis 2:9 speaks of "trees that were pleasing to the eye" (NIV). The cedar in Lebanon has "beautiful branches" (Ezek 31:3 NIV). The lover in the Song of Songs compares his beautiful beloved with the stately palm tree (Song 7:7). The protective shade of a leafy tree is a place of security and rest. The beloved delights to sit in the shade of her lover, who is likened to a fruit-laden apple tree (Song 2:3). Nebuchadnezzar was described in Daniel's interpretation of the king's vision as an enormous tree, whose branches had beautiful leaves, and which bore abundant fruit and gave shelter to the beasts of the field and nesting places for the birds (Dan 4). Similar imagery is seen when the growth of the kingdom of heaven is likened to that of a mustard seed, which from tiny beginnings rapidly shoots up into a great tree that provides shelter for the birds (Mt 13:31). [Dictionary of Biblical Imagery]

"She finds herself feasting on it all. It is as if he is a tree that provides relief from the sun and delicious fruit for her hunger. Her satisfaction lies in him."

Philips notes, "She underlined two things about the apple tree. She was grateful, first, for its protection. She says, "I sat down under his shadow with great delight." Just as, on a hot and humid day, a person will sit down beneath a leafy tree and enjoy the grateful protection it affords from the burning, beating sun, so the Shulamite found her protection in her beloved. Just to sit in the conscious knowledge of his presence, his nearness, his strength, and his protection was heaven to her soul. Surely we do not do that often enough, just simply sit and enjoy Him! He is there to protect us from the burden and heat of the day, when the way becomes wearisome and we feel crushed by the circumstances of life. This is the time when we should deliberately sit down and enjoy Him. Jesus Christ alone supplies the needs of the sons of men. As the apple tree is the exception to the forest trees in bearing its fruit, as it stands on that account in contrast to the trees of the wood, so does Jesus our Beloved contrast with all others, and transcendently excel them: - "An apple tree in simple beauty stands, And waves its juicy treasure gracefully, Among the barren trees which eroded the wood, Of lofty form, but destitute of fruit: So Jesus, 'midst the failing sons of men Bears for my use the fruits of covenant love, And fills my heart with rare delight and rest."

His *Flag* of love was *Flying* over her

He has brought me to his banquet hall, And his banner over me is love.

Banquette laborite meal, sometimes called a "feast." In the OT and NT banquets and feasts are prominent in sealing friendships, celebrating victories, and for other joyous occasions (Dan. 5:1; Luke 15:22-24). The idea of hospitality ran deep in the thought of those in the Near East (Gen. 18:1-8; Luke 11:5-8). Most banquets were held in the evening after the day's work. Usually only men were invited. The women served the food when no servant was present. Hosts sent invitations (Matt. 22:3-4) and sometimes made elaborate preparations for the guests. Those who dined reclined on bedlike seats and lay at right angles to the table. Even though our English translations usually speak of "sitting down" at a meal, the Greek actually means "recline" (Mark 6:39; Luke 12:37). Typical foods served at banquets were fish, bread, olives, various kinds of vegetables, cheeses, honey, dates, and figs. Beef or lamb was used only by the rich or on special occasions (Mark 14:12; Luke 15:23). Wine was also an important part of the feasts, so that they were sometimes called "a house of drinking" in the Hebrew (KJV, "banqueting house," Song 2:4) or "drinkings" in the Greek (KJV, "banquetings," 1 Pet. 4:3). Some "seats" at the banquet table were preferred over others (Mark 10:37; Luke 14:7-11; John 13:23). In Luke 14:8-10 Jesus referred to these "lowest" and "highest" places. He often used banquets and feasts to present His message to various people (Matt. 9:9-10; Mark 14:1-9; Luke 7:36-50; 19:1-6; John 2:1-11; 12:1-8). The image of the feast as an occasion of celebrating victory is seen in Jesus' reference to the messianic banquet (Matt. 8:11; Luke 13:29). Also, in Revelation, the final victory day is described in terms of a "marriage feast of the Lamb" of God (Rev. 19:9 HCSB). [Holman Illustrated Bible Dictionary] Banner (1.) The flag or banner of the larger kind, serving for three tribes marching together. These standards, of which there were four, were worked with embroidery and beautifully ornamented (Num 1:52; Num 2:2, 3, 10, 18, 25; Song 2:4; Song 6:4, 10). (2.) The flag borne by each separate tribe, of a smaller form. Probably it bore on it the name of the tribe to which it belonged, or some distinguishing device (Num 2:2, 34). (3.) A lofty signal-flag, not carried about, but stationary. It was usually erected on a mountain or other lofty place. As soon as it was seen the war-trumpets were blown (Ps 60:4; Isa 5:26; Isa 11:12; Isa 13:2; Isa 18:3; Isa 30:17; Jer 4:6, 21; Ezek 27:7).(4.) A "sign of fire" (Jer 6:1) was sometimes used as a signal. The banners and ensigns of the Roman army had idolatrous images upon them, and hence they are called the "abomination of desolation" (q.v.). The principal Roman standard, however, was an eagle. See (Mat 24:28; Luke 17:37), where the Jewish nation is compared to a dead body, which the eagles gather together to devour.) God's setting up or giving a banner (Ps 20:5; Ps 60:4; Song 2:4) imports his presence and protection and aid extended to his people. [Illustrated Bible Dictionary: And Treasury of Biblical History, Biography, Geography, Doctrine, and Literature]

"The beloved's praise of her lover reveals three aspects of romantic love that are important to women.

- First, she felt protected by him. Sitting in his shade was a metaphor for protection, not only in the Bible but also in the literature of the ancient Near East. She had worked in the sun (1:6) but now she enjoyed resting under his protection.

- Second, they cultivated the kind of relationship that allowed them to know each other intimately. The word taste expressed a knowledge of someone through intimate personal experience (cf. Ps. 34:8, "Taste and see that the Lord is good").

- Third, the beloved appreciated the fact that Solomon let others see his love for her. As a banner (a military standard) was easily seen by the troops as they marched, so Solomon's love for his beloved was easily seen by anyone who observed their relationship. He was not ashamed of her; instead he delighted in her and it was evident to others. One way he showed this was by taking her to his banquet hall (cf. "table" in Song 1:12) in the palace. These three things—protection by her lover, intimacy with him, and obvious displays and expressions of love from him—are crucial factors that enable a woman to develop a sense of security and self-worth and thereby to enjoy a stable marriage. [The Bible Knowledge Commentary]

The king's banner was a pole with a flag-like clothe attached to it. It revealed the kings protective care and love. It also revealed that he was not ashamed of her. God has fixed His love upon every believer and is not ashamed to call us His own. For both He who sanctifies and those who are being sanctified are all of one, for which reason He is not ashamed to call them brethren, Hebrews 2:11. But now they desire a better, that is, a heavenly country. Therefore God is not ashamed to be called their God, for He has prepared a city for them. Hebrews 11:16.

She is *Faint* or *Fatigue*

5 "Sustain me with raisin cakes, Refresh me with apples, Because I am lovesick. 6 "Let his left hand be under my head And his right hand embrace me."

It is the causative use of the genitive construction meaning, I am sick because of love. ḥālāh is a verb found in seventy-five contexts meaning "be sick (or ill)," as well as related nuances. Literal references to being sick include those in 2 Sam. 13:2 ff.; Ps. 35:13; Ezek. 34:4; Hos. 7:5. ḥālāh is used metaphorically in Prov. 13:12 with reference to "the heart being sick," or being cast down or depressed. Song 2:5 records the emotion of being "sick with love," or overwhelmed." [Expository Dictionary of Bible Words]

"Presumably the woman continues speaking and exclaims that the intensity of her love makes her physically weak. She is exhausted...Love has made her faint. The noun from the verb translated "I am lovesick" denotes a loss of physical strength. She is overwhelmed emotionally and physically by her love for the man. It is a strong statement of the power of love...the woman describes her embrace with the man, though it is best to understand the verse to indicate a wish rather than describing a present reality. Nothing like a loving embrace to help someone get through fatigue."

D. L. Moody once had such an experience. He was in New York City. He had been struggling with God's will for his life for some time. He felt that God was calling him to citywide, nationwide, worldwide evangelism, and he was reluctant to yield. He fought and struggled against the call of God. Then, one day, walking through the streets of New York, he gave in. He tells us the exact spot. It was on the corner of Broadway and Fifth Avenue, one of the busiest thoroughfares of the city. He yielded, the last chain snapped, and am overwhelming sense of the presence of God came flooding over his soul. "God Almighty seemed very near me," he said. "I felt I must be alone." He hurried to the house of a friend and, resisting all offers of food and hospitality, requested a room where he could be alone. "I have an urgent need to be alone," he said. He was shown into a room. He locked the door and sat upon a couch. The room seemed ablaze with the glory of God; it was like the Mount of Transfiguration itself. "I can only say," he wrote later to a friend, "that God revealed Himself to me and I had such an experience of His love that I had to ask Him to stay His hand." A clock in a nearby tower chimed away the hours, but Moody was oblivious to time. He was overwhelmed by the love of God. He experienced in the highest, rarest, and most spiritual sense what the Shulamite experienced.

They refuse to *Force* the moment

7 "I adjure you, O daughters of Jerusalem, By the gazelles or by the hinds of the field, That you do not arouse or awaken my love Until she pleases." - "She warns them not to awaken or arouse love until it desires. But what exactly is the warning against? One suggest that it is like putting out a "do not disturb sign." More naturally, she is, in essence, telling them not to force it.
Wait for love to blossom; don't hurry it. We too are to learn the same lesson: Wait for love

to blossom; don't try to stimulate it artificially. After all, in the proceeding verses we have seen that love takes it toll on the woman. She warns the others not to arouse love until they are ready to meet its rigors, both physical and emotional. Love is not a passing fling but rather a demanding and exhausting relationship." [Longman]

Premarital purity is clearly demanded in this book: 3:5; 4:12; 8:4, 8-12.

As one noted, "Love does not trespass where law forbids. It is lust, not love that does that kind of thing. Love knows how to behave itself, where to draw the line, where to observe its proper bounds. Love knows where to draw the line, where to recognize the boundaries between right and wrong. Lust blunders on into sin, but love observes God's laws. This, indeed, is how this section of the Song concludes. It puts an end to the sordid speculations of those who would see something improper in the preceding verse. For true love does not ravish; it does not eat of the forbidden fruit. Love knows how to wait and how to keep itself pure. We notice, then, love's boundary..."Stir not up!" The thought is "excite not!" "Awake!" The Hebrew word means "to incite!" The Shulamite is not saying that neither she nor her beloved are to be awakened from sleep. She is saying that her passions are not to be excited, awakened, or stirred up...It is a lesson that needs very much to be underlined today. We are living in an age when passion is for sale. Erotic books, magazines, and films are everywhere being thrust upon us. The great tempter knows how to arouse passion. We need to draw the line and draw it with a firm, deliberate hand by refusing to consider for a single moment things that would awaken desire illicitly."

He is on *Fast-forward*

8 "Listen! My beloved! Behold, he is coming, Climbing on the mountains, Leaping on the hills! 9 "My beloved is like a gazelle or a young stag. Behold, he is standing behind our wall, He is looking through the windows, He is peering through the lattice. - notice all of these animals. MacArthur Study Bible has a good chart identifying all these animals and things.The point is, he is excited! He not just running but he is leaping and skipping. Like the gazelle [an antelope type animal] and a young stag [a young male deer] who are known for their speed, this guy is on fast-forward! He has so much energy that he is like superman - he can leap tall buildings with a single bound. He comes to the woman's home, stares through the window, and call for her to come out to him.

It is the *Favored* time for love

¹⁰ *"My beloved responded and said to me, 'Arise, my darling, my beautiful one, And come along.* ¹¹ *'For behold, the winter is past, The rain is over and gone.* ¹² *'The flowers have already appeared in the land; The time has arrived for pruning the vines, And the voice of the turtledove has been heard in our land.* ¹³ *'The fig tree has ripened its figs, And the vines in blossom have given forth their fragrance. Arise, my darling, my beautiful one, And come along!'"*

Winter is gone and spring has arrived - it is spring fever! Springtime is the universal time for love - warmer weather, the smell of flowers, a time to get outside and enjoy the many sights and sounds!

Spurgeon, "I have had winters of dark trouble, succeeded by soft springs of deliverance. We have had our Gethsemanes, when our souls have been exceeding sorrowful; nothing could comfort us, but then at last, the Comforter came to us, and all of our troubles dissipated and we finally began to sing. The great temporal affliction which had crushed us was suddenly removed, and the strong temptation of Satan was taken off from us. The deep depression of spirit which threatened to drive us to insanity was all of a sudden lifted off, and we once again like David, danced before the ark."

He is calling her to come out of her *Fortress*

14 "O my dove, in the clefts of the rock, In the secret place of the steep pathway, Let me see your form, Let me hear your voice; For your voice is sweet, And your form is lovely." - Being virtually defenseless, they would often take refuge in crevices and cliffs for safety (Jer 48:28). The emphasis on timidity and the need for security is undoubtedly the emphasis here because of the explicit description of this "dove" hiding in the "clefts of the rock" and in "the hiding places of the mountain crevice." Fortresses were sometimes built in the clefts of the rocks on mountainsides because they were inaccessible and therefore, in a secure place of safety (Jer 49:16; Obad 3). Perhaps he realized it might be intimidating for her to join him and communicate with him freely. She would need to feel secure in his love to do this. It would be easy for her to hide from such emotionally exposing experiences. [NET Bible]

Don't be detoured by the little *Foxes*

"Catch the foxes for us, The little foxes that are ruining the vineyards, While our vineyards are in blossom." - "The idea is that there are foxes running lose in the vineyard destroying the fruit. Foxes in that day were known pests, they are used in a general sense for anything that seek to disrupt their relationship, any obstacle - these obstacles will not be allowed to deter their love. One obstacle would be other men, who would seek to captivate the young Shulamite woman as she is roaming about looking for her lover."

In Egyptian love poetry foxes represent sexually aggressive men, rather like the term "wolf" in American idiom.

There is a commitment to mutual *Faithfulness*

[16] *"My beloved is mine, and I am his; He pastures his flock among the lilies.* [17] *"Until the cool of the day when the shadows flee away, Turn, my beloved, and be like a gazelle Or a young stag on the mountains of Bether."* - They exchange the language of ownership, she belongs to him, and he belongs to her.

Now I belong to Jesus,
Jesus belongs to me;
Not for the years of time alone
But for eternity.

How do we belong to God? *Like a bride belongs to the bridegroom*. In fact, the Bible often uses the intimacies between husband and wife to illustrate our union with the Lord. In Ephesians 5, Paul's description of the marriage relationship, he concludes by saying, "This is a profound mystery—but I am talking about Christ and the church."
We belong to him in the most exalted and personal way—*like sheep to a shepherd*. Jesus said, "I am the good shepherd; I know my sheep and my sheep know me—just as the Father knows me and I know the Father" (John 10:14-15a). We also belong to him *like a child belongs to his father*.

When Alan Redpath's two daughters were younger, he heard his wife say, "Girls, go get your father for breakfast." The oldest bounded up the steps, and by the time the youngest (who was considerably younger) made it to the room puffing from the race, her big sister said, "I have already told Daddy breakfast is ready, and besides I have all of Daddy." The little one took that pronouncement hard, and a tear began to run down her cheek, so her father sat her on his knee. She put her head on his shoulder, then smiled big and said to her sister, "You might have all of Daddy, but Daddy has all of me." Paul was his Father's possession, and that truth so permeated his inner being that he described God as "the God whose I am."

We belong to God *because he bought us*.

[19] Or do you not know that your body is a temple of the Holy Spirit who is in you, whom you have from God, and that you are not your own? [20] For you have been bought with a price: therefore glorify God in your body. 1 Corinthians 6:19-20

Paul traced God's possession of him not to the fact that God is Creator, but to the one transcendent act of divine love in which Christ gave his life to purchase us for himself.

Her *Frantic* search for him

[1] "On my bed night after night I sought him Whom my soul loves; I sought him but did not find him. [2] 'I must arise now and go about the city; In the streets and in the squares I must seek him whom my soul loves.' I sought him

but did not find him. ³ "The watchmen who make the rounds in the city found me, And I said, 'Have you seen him whom my soul loves?'

Deere notes, "The phrase 'By night on my bed' indicates that the experience she was describing took place in a dream. When a person loves another person deeply, it is natural to fear losing him or her. In her dream she lost her lover and sought to find him...In her dream she went to a city to look for him, but she was unsuccessful. She even asked the watchmen, men who guarded the city at night, if they had seen him. Apparently they had not."

Ironside observes, "For though the soul loses the sense of His presence, nevertheless, He still abides faithful. He never forsakes His people though He seems to have withdrawn and He does not manifest Himself...She must seek until she finds; she cannot be contented without him. Would that this were always true of us! She must find him who is all in all to her. Only the sense of his presence can satisfy her heart. Nothing gives our Lord more delight, than to find a heart that joys in Him for what He is in Himself. Too often we think rather of His gifts."

The bride's eyes not her garments,
But her dear Bridegroom's face;
I will not gaze at glory,
But on my King of Grace!
Not at the crown He giveth,
But on His pierced Hand;
The Lamb is all the glory
Of Immanuel's land.

She finally *Finds* Him

4 "Scarcely had I left them When I found him whom my soul loves; I held on to him and would not let him go Until I had brought him to my mother's house, And into the room of her who conceived me." 5 "I adjure you, O daughters of Jerusalem, By the gazelles or by the hinds of the field, That you will not arouse or awaken my love Until she pleases."

One writes, "This is the first of the second series of steps, *"I found him."* I do not wish to stand here, and speak for myself alone; but I want, beloved, that you should each one of you also say, "I love him," "I sought him," and now, "I have found him." Notice what the spouse said, "I found him." She was not satisfied with finding anything else: "I found him." If she had found her nearest and dearest friend, if the mother of whom she speaks had met her, it would not have sufficed. She had said, "I love him, I sought him," and she must be able to add, "I found him." Nothing but Christ consciously enjoyed can satisfy the craving of a loving heart which once sets out to seek the King in his beauty.

The city watchmen found the spouse, and she spoke to them; she enquired of them, "Saw ye him whom my soul loveth?" She did not sit down, and say to any one of them, "O watchman of the night, thy company cheers me! The streets are lonely and dangerous; but if thou art near, I feel perfectly safe, and I will be content to stay awhile with thee." Nay, but she leaves the watchmen, and still goes along the streets until she finds him whom her soul loveth. I have known some, who love the Lord, to be very happy while the preacher is proclaiming the truth to them; but they have stopped with the preacher, and have gone no further. This will never do, dear friends; do not be content to abide with us, who are only watchmen, but go beyond us, and seek till you find our Master. I should groan in heart, indeed, if any of you believed simply because of my word, as if it were my word alone that led you to believe, or if you should look merely to me for anything you need for your soul. In myself, I am nothing, and I have nothing; I only watch that, if I can, I may lead you to my

Lord, whose shoe-latches I am not worthy to unloose. O you who love Christ, go beyond the means of grace! Go beyond ordinances, go beyond preachers, go beyond even the Bible itself, into an actual possession of the living Christ; labor after a conscious enjoyment of Jesus himself, till you can say with the spouse, *"I found him whom my soul loveth."* It is good to find sound doctrine, for it is very scarce nowadays. It is good to learn the practical precepts of the gospel, it is good to be in the society of the saints; but if you put any of these in the place of communion with your Lord himself, you do ill. Never be content till you can say, "I found him." Dear souls, did you ever find him? Have you yet found him? If you have not, keep on seeking, keep on praying, till at last you can say, "Eureka! I have found him whom my soul loveth. Jesus is indeed mine."

The grand *Finale*

6 "What is this coming up from the wilderness Like columns of smoke, Perfumed with myrrh and frankincense, With all scented powders of the merchant? 7 "Behold, it is the traveling couch of Solomon; Sixty mighty men around it, Of the mighty men of Israel. 8 "All of them are wielders of the sword, Expert in war; Each man has his sword at his side, Guarding against the terrors of the night. ⁹ "King Solomon has made for himself a sedan chair From the timber of Lebanon. ¹⁰ "He made its posts of silver, Its back of gold And its seat of purple fabric, With its interior lovingly fitted out By the daughters of Jerusalem. ¹¹ "Go forth, O daughters of Zion, And gaze on King Solomon with the crown With which his mother has crowned him On the day of his wedding, And on the day of his gladness of heart."

A central feature of a wedding ceremony was a procession to the bride's home led by the groom, who then escorted her back to their new residence. Next, a wedding feast was given which lasted up to a week or even longer. The couple consummated their marriage on the first night of the feast.

Philip gives a good overview, "How wonderful! The Lord always reveals Himself to those who truly love Him, just when they need Him most. Picture the scene! First there was the dream with its nightmare qualities followed by the awakening. Then came the midnight search through the darkened streets filled with fears and alarms only to be followed by the frightening and embarrassing encounter with the guard. Then the sudden sight of her beloved! No wonder she seized him and would not let him go!

It is all very true to life. We see Mary Magdalene alone in the garden on the resurrection morn, staring forlornly at the empty tomb. His death was dreadful...then suddenly she heard a sound. She wheeled around, and there in the glory of the morn stood a man! The stranger spoke a word, just one word: Mary! In a moment, the scales fell from her eyes. She knew Him! It was the Lord!"

This life gets dreary and we often long for a closer intimacy with the Lord. One day suddenly, we will wheel around, and hear a voice saying, "Come up here!" And we will see our Lord face to face!!!

Spurgeon, "We should seek to love as God has loved us, but to the infinite, boundless degree, we shall never arrive. There is no love like the love of God in Christ. It is love which to us has become this day our brightest thought; our truest comfort; and our most potent incentive. The ungodly, if they do right after a fashion, do it from fear of punishment but the true born children of God are obedient, not because they hope to get to heaven by their good works - they have heaven already by the works of another, guaranteed to them by the promise of God: but they serve God out of pure gratitude for what they have received, rejoicing as they work in the service of One, they love so well."

CHAPTER THREE

THE CONSUMMATION

Him (to her): 1You, my love, are beautiful. So beautiful! Your eyes are like doves nestled behind your veil. Your hair moves as gracefully as a flock of goats leaping down the slopes of Mount Gilead. 2Your teeth are pearl white like a flock of sheep shorn, fresh up from a wash. Each perfect and paired with another; not one of them is lost. 3Your lips are as red as scarlet threads; your mouth is beautiful. Your cheeks rosy and round are beneath your veil, like the halves of a pomegranate. 4Your neck is elegant like the tower of David, perfectly fit stone-by-stone. There hang a thousand shields, the shields of mighty men. 5Your breasts are like two fawns, twin gazelles grazing in a meadow of lilies. 6As the day breathes its morning breeze and shadows turn and flee, I will go up your myrrh mountain and climb your frankincense hill. 7You are so beautiful, my love, without blemish. 8Come with me from Lebanon, my bride; come with me from Lebanon. Journey with me from the crest of Amana, from the top of Senir even the summit of Hermon, From the lions' dangerous den, from the mountain hideouts of leopards. 9My heart is your captive, my sister, my bride; you have stolen it with one glance, caught it with a single strand of your necklace. 10How beautiful is your love, my sister, my bride! Your love is more pleasing than the finest wine, and the fragrance of your perfume brings more delight than any spice! 11Your lips taste sweet like honey off the comb, my bride; milk and honey are beneath your tongue. The scents of your clothes are like the fresh air of Lebanon. 12You are a locked garden, my sister, my bride, open only to me; a spring closed up tight, a sealed fountain. 13Your sprouts are an orchard of pomegranates and exotic fruits— with henna and nard, 14With nard and saffron, calamus and cinnamon— With rows of frankincense trees and myrrh and aloes and all the finest spices. 15My bride, you are a fountain in a garden, a well of life-giving water flowing down from Lebanon.

Him (to the winds): 16Rise, you north wind; come, you south wind. Breathe on my garden, and let the fragrance of its natural spices fill the air.

Her: Let my love come into his garden and feast from its choice fruits. [Voice Bible]

Spurgeon, "I do not know how to preach this subject. Who can? Is it a subject for exposition in a mixed assembly? If it were, who could compass it? I beg you, O believer, to sit in your pew, and let holy thoughts occupy you: if you are a true believer, the point is that He has brought you into a condition of the utmost conceivable nearness with Himself."

I feel like apologizing ahead of time for such a graphic message, but then, how does one apologize for the Word of God?

The *FOREPLAY* - the Talk

He compliments her *Brown* eyes - remember she is Jewish

"How beautiful you are, my darling, How beautiful you are! Your eyes are like doves behind your veil - Remember that old song, "You my brown-eyed girl?"

"Doves were associated with love in the ancient world, appearing as literal messengers of love in Egyptian art. Shulamith's eyes were messengers of love to Solomon."

The veil - hides beauty and heightens desire to unveil! If a woman went topless 24/7 before long no one would really care! Look at an old National Geographic and you will see women running around exposed and few give it much protest.

He admires her long flowing *Black* hair

Your hair is like a flock of goats That have descended from Mount Gilead - Most Palestinian goats have wavy long black hair. To say that her hair was like a flock of goats coming down Mount Gilead (cf. 6:5) hardly sounds like a compliment, but it was. Seen from a distance the dark hair of Palestinian goats was beautiful in the sunset as a flock was descending from the mountains. The beloved's dark hair had the same beautiful quality. Mount Gilead was a mountain range east of the Jordan River in Gilead, known for its fertile pastures and many flocks (cf. Micah 7:14).

He is impressed with her *Beautiful* glistening teeth

"Your teeth are like a flock of newly shorn ewes Which have come up from their washing, All of which bear twins, And not one among them has lost her young - Her teeth were straight, even, white, and none missing! It is important to understand the dental hygiene was nothing like it is today, teeth in that day

were commonly decayed, missing, and jagged.

She has *Bright* red lips and cheeks

Your lips are like a scarlet thread, And your mouth is lovely. Your temples are like a slice of a pomegranate Behind your veil - Her lips are brilliantly red. Thread, may either express the idea of thinness, which is unlikely, or it may indicate that her mouth is very clearly defined as by a fine thread. Like a woman wearing red lipstick today.

She has a *Bull* neck - just kidding! Her neck is *Becoming*.

Your neck is like the tower of David, Built with rows of stones on which are hung a thousand shields, all the round shields of the mighty men - In Scripture the neck is sometimes associated with beauty or prosperity, although in itself it is usually less prominent than the jewelry that adorns it (Gen 41:42; Judg 5:30; Prov 1:9). However, in Song of Songs 4:4 and 7:4 the lover praises his beloved's neck itself, rather than the jewelry she wears, making her the focus of his love. In the cultures of the ancient Near East, neck ornaments were worn as a sign of authority, status or beauty by high officials (Gen 41:42; Dan 5:7, 16, 29), by women (Is 3:18; Ezek 16:11) and even by camels (Judg 8:21). The author of the prologue of Proverbs appears to employ this custom as a metaphor for accepting parental instruction as a source of honor and blessing (Prov 1:9; 3:3, 22; 6:21).

We do not exactly know what the tower of David was, but her neck was like a beautiful necklace, which spoke of dignity and elegance.

She had beautiful *Breasts*

Your two breasts are like two fawns, Twins of a gazelle Which feed among the lilies. 6 "Until the cool of the day When the shadows flee away, I will go my way to the mountain of myrrh And to the hill of frankincense. - They were young, firm, soft, and perky.

Solomon extols the qualities of the breasts of the beloved woman (Song 4:5; 7:3; 8:10). Proverbs encourages the young man to restrict his sexual activities to his own wife: "May her breasts satisfy you at all times" (Prov 5:19). On the one hand, the images convey a very positive attitude toward the pleasures and comforts of sex as God-given; and on the other hand, a clear condemnation of promiscuous behavior as a misuse of sex. Hosea longs for his wife to "put away...her adultery from between her breasts" (Hos 2:2

NRSV). The used of "mountain" and "hill" are metaphors for her breasts.

She has no *Blemishes*

You are altogether beautiful, my darling, And there is no blemish in you - A specific Hebrew term meaning "blemish," mûm occurs approximately twenty times and is found mostly in the legislative sections of the Pentateuch. References to physical blemishes or imperfections on Israelite people are mentioned in Lev. 21:17 ff. These physical flaws bar those afflicted from worshiping at the tabernacle while the conditions persist. Lev. 22:20 ff.; Deut. 15:21; 17:1 refer to prohibited offerings in which the prospective animals for sacrifice are to be rejected because of certain physical imperfections. In a unique use of mûm, Num. 19:2 refers to a red heifer "without blemish" as the required sin offering for the Israelite community. See below under tāmîm for a full discussion of the phrase "without blemish."
mûm also refers to physical beauty in terms of the absence of blemish. This is predicated, for example, of Absalom (cf. 2 Sam. 14:25); the Shulamite's lover and husband in Song 4:7; and the Israelite youths deported to Babylon from Israel by Nebuchadnezzar at the very end of the sixth century B.C. (Dan. 1:4). This group included Daniel and his three

friends Hananiah, Mishael, and Azariah.

On three occasions mûm indicates "blemish" in a moral sense. First, Deut. 32:5 refers to God's people as "tarnished" or "blemished" by their sin against God. In Job 11:15, Zophar declares to Job that if he puts away sin that is in his hand, he will be able to lift up his face "without blemish" (i.e., without shame). And finally, Prov. 9:7 mentions that whoever rebukes a wicked person will incur "abuse" from him or her.

He *Beckons* her to let him in

Come with me from Lebanon, my bride, May you come with me from Lebanon. Journey down from the summit of Amana, From the summit of Senir and Hermon, From the dens of lions, From the mountains of leopards - The previous sexual distance is now over.

He *Begins* praising her again

⁹ "You have made my heart beat faster, my sister, my bride; You have made my heart beat faster with a single glance of your eyes, With a single strand of your necklace. ¹⁰ "How beautiful is your love, my sister, my bride! How much better is your love than wine, And the fragrance of your oils Than all kinds of spices! ¹¹ "Your lips, my bride, drip honey;

Honey and milk are under your tongue, And the fragrance of your garments is like the fragrance of Lebanon

He is *Bursting* at the seams - *"You have made my heart beat faster"*

She is his *Buddy - Sister,* was a common term of endearment in the love poetry of the ancient Near East" [Archaeological Study Bible]

She is now his *Bride - "my bride"*

He is going *Bonkers - with a single glance of your eyes, With a single strand of your necklace*

He is a hunk, a hunk of *Burning* love - *"How beautiful is your love, my sister, my bride! How much better is your love than wine,*

She's a *Bed* of roses - *And the fragrance of your oils Than all kinds of spices!*

He is going Bananas - *Your lips, my bride, drip honey; Honey and milk are under your tongue, And the fragrance of your garments is like the fragrance of Lebanon* This is foreplay!

He focuses on the garden *Between* her legs

¹² "A garden locked is my sister, my bride, A rock garden locked, a spring sealed up. ¹³ "Your shoots are an orchard of pomegranates With choice fruits, henna with nard plants, ¹⁴ Nard and saffron, calamus and cinnamon, With all the trees of frankincense, Myrrh and aloes, along with all the finest spices. ¹⁵ "You are a garden spring, A well of fresh water, And streams flowing from Lebanon." ¹⁶ "Awake, O north wind, And come, wind of the south; Make my garden breathe out fragrance, Let its spices be wafted abroad. May my beloved come into his garden And eat its choice fruits!" - "Garden, the Hebrew means "a covered or hidden place." In biblical times a garden was a walled enclosure, a place of shade and refreshment. The shulamite's garden, a reference to her intimate sexual organs, is the absolute and sole possession of the bridegroom. The phrase "a spring shut up" refers to the sealed fountain protected from all impurity in a country in which water was scarce. No one could approach the "fountain" except its owner. Their relationship was to be exclusive. The fact that Solomon evidently violated this does not change the divine design." [Baptist Study Bible]

"Blow upon my garden" expresses the desire that her fragrance be blown about to draw her lover to her so that they can enjoy love's intimacies." [Archaeological Study Bible]

"The image of the garden behind its walls and with the gate locked suggests the unapproach- ableness of the area to all but those who rightfully belong. Metaphorically the "garden" is used as a euphemism for the female sexual organs and here, a fountain sealed and a garden locked speaks of virginity." [Carr]

THE NO LONGER *FORBIDDEN PLEASURE*

Him (to her): 1I have come into my garden, my sister, my bride; I have gathered my myrrh with its natural spices. I have tasted the honeycomb dripping with my honey and have drunk my wine and milk together. (to his young friends of Jerusalem) Eat, friends, drink your fill! Be intoxicated with love.

I have come into my garden, my sister, my bride; I have gathered my myrrh along with my balsam. I have eaten my honeycomb and my honey; I have drunk my wine and my milk. Eat, friends; Drink and imbibe deeply, O lovers.

The two *become* one

God's *Blessing* is on them

Who but God would have been present in the bedroom on their wedding night! God voice's His pleasure and approval of the sexual union within the confines of marriage.

Josh McDowell, "Let's clear up one misconception. God is pro-sex! He invented sex and thinks it's beautiful when enjoyed within the correct framework. Proverbs tells us "Take pleasure in the wife of your youth...let her breasts always satisfy you; be lost in her love." [Prov. 5:18-19]. The context in proverbs is speaking of sex within the parameters of a lifelong marriage commitment.
Another example of God's perspective on sex is the Song of Songs, an OT book that uses the beauty of the sexual experience to express one's spiritual experience. The truth is, I haven't been able to locate a single verse in the Bible that decries sex as sinful, dirty, or wrong. It's only the misuse of sex that is wrong. Sex as God intended it, is a beautiful thing."

In fact Paul warns, "5 Do not deprive one another except with consent for a time, that you may give yourselves to fasting and prayer; and come together again so that Satan does not tempt you because of your lack of self-control. 6 But I say this as a concession, not as a commandment. 1 Corinthians 7:5-6

As one put it, "Here, then, the gist of the whole matter. The Master's presence is in the church in a very remarkable manner. Beloved I pray that none of you may be like Adam, who fled among the trees to hide himself from God when He walked in the garden. He calls you, O backslider, He calls you as He once called Adam: "Where are you?" Come, behold and commune with your Lord. Let none of us be like the disciples in another garden, when their Lord was there, and He was in agony, but they were sleeping.
Up you sleepers for Christ has come. Get up you slumberers, and now with heart and soul seek fellowship with Him. It would be a sad thing if while was with Christ us, any of us should wake up and say, "Surely God was in this place, and I knew it not."

CHAPTER FOUR

CONFLICT

Her: 2I was sleeping, but my heart was awake when I heard a sound, the sound of my love pounding at the door.
Him: Open yourself to me, my sister, my dearest, my sweet dove, my flawless beauty. My head is drenched with dew; my hair is soaked with the wetness of the night.
Her: 3I have taken off my robe. How could I ever put it on again? I have washed my feet. How could I walk across this dirty floor? 4My love put his hand on the latch; my insides began to throb for him. 5I leaped from my bed to let my love in. My hands were dripping sweet myrrh, My fingers were coated with myrrh as I reached for the handles of the lock. 6I opened for my love, but he had turned away and was gone. He'd left, and my heart sank. I looked for him, but I did not see him. I called out to him, but he did not answer. 7The watchmen found me as they made their rounds in the city. They beat me, they left bruises on my skin, and they took away my veil, those watchmen on the walls. 8(to the young women of Jerusalem) Promise me that if you find my love, you will speak with him, telling him that I am faint with love.

Young Women of Jerusalem: 9How is your beloved better than all the other lovers, most beautiful of women? How is your beloved worth more than all the rest, that you would make us promise this?
Her: 10Because my love is radiant and ruddy, he stands out above 10,000 other men. 11His head is pure gold; his hair is thick and wavy and black as a raven. 12His eyes are like doves at the edge of a stream, mounted like jewels and bathed in pools of milk. 13His bearded cheeks are like a spice garden, with towers of spice: His lips are lilies dripping and flowing with myrrh, 14His hands are like strong rods of gold, each set with jewels. His body displays his manhood like an ivory tusk inlaid with sapphires. 15His legs are like pillars of white marble, both set on bases of gold. He stands tall and strong like the mountains of Lebanon, with all its majestic cedars. 16His mouth tastes sweet, so sweet; he is altogether desirable. This is my love. This is my dear one, as I am his, O young women of Jerusalem.
Young Women of Jerusalem (to her): 1Where has your love gone, most beautiful of women? Do you know which direction he went so we can help you find him?
Her: 2Women of Jerusalem, I know where my love is. My love has gone into his garden Among the beds of aromatic spices, like a gazelle grazing among his gardens and a

gardener gathering the lilies. 3I belong to my love, and my love to me. He feeds his flock among the lilies.

Him (to her): 4You are beautiful, my dear, as beautiful as Tirzah, as lovely as Jerusalem, as regal as an army beneath their banners. 5Turn your eyes from me because they overpower me as always. Your hair moves as gracefully as a flock of goats leaping down the slopes of Mount Gilead. 6Your teeth are pearl white like a flock of sheep shorn, fresh up from a wash. Each is perfect and paired with another; not one of them is lost. 7Your cheeks are rosy and round beneath your veil, like the halves of a pomegranate. 8There may be 60 queens and 80 concubines— there may be more virgins than can be counted— 9But my dove, my perfect love is the only one for me, the only daughter of her mother, the pure and favored child to the one who bore her. The young women saw her and called her blessed; the queens and concubines praised her.

Young Women of Jerusalem: 10Who is this who looks down like the dawn, as radiant as the full moon, as bright as sunlight, as majestic as an army beneath their banners?

Her: 11I went down to walk among a stand of walnut trees, to take in the new growth of the valley, To see if the vines had budded or the pomegranates were blooming. 12Before I

knew it, my passions set me before some chariots, those belonging to my noble people.
Young Women of Jerusalem: 13Come back, come back, O Shulammite! Come back, come back to us, so that we can look upon you.
Him: Why should you look upon the Shulammite, as you would stare at the dance of joyous victory at Mahanaim? [Voice Bible]

"The Bride was there at night, asleep in her bed. She heard the voice of the bridegroom, calling for her to open. I think there are times when the Lord is calling us into fellowship, longing for that close intimacy. "Spend some time with Me," He says. I wonder how many times we just pass it off, when God is calling to us. "Lord, I'm too busy right now. Lord I need my sleep. I have a busy day tomorrow."

We need to respond to the Lord, because if we don't we will quench the Spirit, and getting back into fellowship, is not as easy as some might think.

Her Questionable Slumber

She should be *Awake!*

I was asleep but my heart was awake. A voice! My beloved was knocking: 'Open to me, my sister, my darling, My dove, my perfect one! For my head is drenched with dew, My locks with the damp of the night.' - "Sleep is a state of inaction. It does not pray and thus will sooner or later hear the Masters voice say, "Could you not stay awake and watch with me for even one hour?" He will hear Paul thunder, "It's high time to wake out of our sleep, for we are not children of the night, but of the day." We are often admonished in Scripture to be alert, awake, waiting and ready for the master to return. Nothing can be more inexcusable than for us to sleep, seeing that we are not of the night nor of darkness. If we had been the children of the night, it might seem according to our nature for us to be sluggards."

She is *Aware* of her condition

"Her sleep is a state recognized. When a person can say "I sleep" they are not altogether steeped in slumber. It is good when God's people can say with grief, "I sleep," the lost overcome with spiritual death, have no consciousness of their state. It is a tender, hopeful conscience that is aware that it is a sleep!"

"What Did Hinder You?" Gal. 5:7
"The water is not hot for the bath." So said a servant maid, after the fire in the kitchen grate had been burning for some hours, and in

calling attention to what she said was the cause, she held up a piece of coal, and said the coal went to a cinder soon after it was lighted! Attention was drawn by her mistress to the fact, "There is a fire sufficient to roast an ox!" That was an exaggeration, but there was certainly fire enough to roast a joint. The reason why the water did not get hot was not with the coal, but with the maid, for the flue at the back, in front of the boiler was found to be choked with ashes. When the flue was cleared, the fire could get under the boiler, and soon there was hot water enough and to spare. We often blame effects when we should deal with causes. When the causes are adjusted the effects are of benefit. How many hindrances there are which affect the Christian life and hinder its developments!

1. The *lack of adding* the graces of the Spirit will hinder us from seeing "afar off"—2 Peter 1:9.

2. The *want of diligence* will keep us out of God's resting rest—Heb. 4:1-6, R.V.

3. The *failure to "go on* to perfection" will cause us to be babes in the Christian life—Heb. 3:12;6:1.

4. The *"carnal" state of half-heartedness* will keep us back from the realm of spirituality—1 Cor. 3:1-3.

5. The *sleepiness of a slothful state* will cause Christ to depart from us, when we might have enjoyed His fellowship—Song of Solomon 5:1-6.

6. The *spirit of legality* will cause us to be left out of the liberty of grace—Gal. 5:1.

7. The *giving heed to the fables* and fancies of men will mar our testimony in the Lord's service—1 Tim. 1:3-19.

[1000 Bible Study Outlines: Study Helps and Sermon Outlines]

He arrives to *Quench* his thirst

He makes the *Initiation*

He *comes* to her - *I was asleep but my heart was awake. A voice! My beloved was knocking...*

He *Calls* out to her - 'Open to me, my sister, my darling, My dove, my perfect one! For my head is drenched with dew, My locks with the damp of the night.'

He *Continues* – He continues knocking is the tense.

He *Compliments* - no matter what she does, he never stops complimenting.

She is *Precious* to him - *my sister*, "Although the Mosaic law forbade marriage between a brother and sister, there were a few cases of such marriages before God gave Moses the law (Lev 18:11). Genesis seems to imply that Cain and Abel married their sisters of necessity, since there was no one else for them to marry. Abraham marries Sarah, his half-sister, with whom he shared a common father (Gen 20:12). Later Amram, Moses's father, married his father's sister Jochabed (Ex 6:20). Even after men ceased to marry their sisters, *sister* was an affectionate term for a husband to call his wife, and the beloved in the Song of Songs even goes so far as to wish that her lover were her brother so she could kiss him in public (Song 5:1; 8:1). Thus although marriage between brothers and sisters was forbidden, the closeness of a brother-sister relationship came to metaphorically represent the relationship of a husband and wife."

my darling – i.e., his love.

1. Love is the *Oil to lubricate* all our spiritual being, and to cause it to run easily—1 Cor. 13:4-8.

2. Love is the *Life to rejuvenate*, so that everything may blossom fruitfully—John 15:10-16.

3. Love is the *Affection to captivate,* and to cause us to go with others willingly—Ruth 1:16, 17.

4. Love is the *Power to consecrate,* which causes us to sacrifice ardently—1 Sam. 18:3, 4.

5. Love is the *Spring to animate,* which will cause us to do something for the benefit of others—1 Chron. 11:17-19.

6. Love is a *Tonic to stimulate,* to give wings to our feet in service—John 20:4.

7. Love is the *Grace to elevate,* to lift us above the plain of self—Gal. 2:20.

my dove - Because of the dove's softness, beauty of feathers and eyes, and affection for and faithfulness to its mate, Song of Songs several times likens the lover to a dove (e.g., Song 1:15;2:14; 4:1; 5:2, 12; 6:9). [Dictionary of Biblical Imagery]

She is *Perfect* to him - *my perfect one! tām* is an adjective meaning "blameless." It may also be translated "perfect," but not in the sense of one who is without sin. "Blamelessness" in Scripture is a quality predicated of those who manifest a godly character, moral integrity, or uprightness. In one or two instances, *tām* refers to that which is perceived as "perfect" in the sense of "flawless." *tām* is found thirteen times. The attribute of being "perfect," in the sense of one who is morally upright is applied, for example, to Job in Job 1:1, 8; 2:3; 9:21. General references to those who are "blameless," "morally upright" are found in Job 8:20; 9:20, 22; Pss. 37:37; 64:4; Prov. 29:10. The man refers to his beloved partner in the Song of Songs as "perfect," or flawless in beauty (Song 5:2; 6:9). [Expository Dictionary of Bible Words]

His *Complaints*

- He's been Waiting *Long* for her - *For my head is covered with dew* -
His *head* and *hair* were covered *with dew,* as he had been outside. Dew in Israel was often heavy.

- It's been Raining Lightly outside - *My locks with the drops of the night...*

She *Quenches* his efforts

I have taken off my dress, How can I put it on again? I have washed my feet, how can I dirty them again? - these are obviously flimsy excuses.

McGee notes, "Actually, that is one of those little foxes which destroy the grapes. We lose our fellowship when we step out of the will of God. That is what it means to quench the Spirit (see 1Thess. 5:19). It is quenching the Spirit to refuse to go where He wants us to go or to do what He wants us to do...There are a great many Christians who have done one of two things: they have grieved the Spirit by sin in their lives, or they have quenched the Spirit by not being obedient [and responsive] to the Lord. That breaks fellowship with Him and causes us to lose our joy. It does not mean that we lose our salvation, but the joy of our salvation."

Her *Quantum* Leap

⁴ "My beloved extended his hand through the opening, And my feelings were aroused for him. ⁵ "I arose to open to my beloved; And my hands dripped with myrrh, And my fingers with liquid myrrh, On the handles of the bolt - "In our modern vernacular, we would say that she had given him "the brush-off." As swift as a flash, she was covered with shame. Thank God for such a swift and sensitive response to the sudden loss of fellowship! Would that we, too, were more alert to the loss! She had raised a barrier, however, and that barrier was not to be thus easily torn down. [John Phillips Commentary Series]

His *Quick* departure

I opened to my beloved, But my beloved had turned away and had gone! My heart went out to him as he spoke. I searched for him but I did not find him; I called him but he did not answer me - we don't come to God on our own terms, our time-table, our personal whims. When He speaks and we stiff arm Him and say, "I'll get back with you at a convenient Lord!" we definitely grieve the Spirit.

Her *Quest*

My heart went out to him as he spoke. I searched for him but I did not find him; I called him but he did not answer me - How many of us are seeking revival, simply because we refuse to take it when it was offered?

The *Quandary* [predicament]

7 "The watchmen who make the rounds in the city found me, They struck me and wounded me; The guardsmen of the walls took away my shawl from me. 8 "I adjure you, O daughters of Jerusalem, If you find my beloved, As to what you will tell him: For I am lovesick." - There is not only chastisement for sins of commission, but also of omission. Not responding to God's voice, is just as sinful as responding to Satan's voice!

If she had responded to Him, she would not have been wandering all over the city! They took her for a prostitute?

The *Question*

The *Charge* - "I adjure you, O daughters of Jerusalem, If you find my beloved, As to what you will tell him: For I am lovesick."

The *Challenge* - What kind of beloved is your beloved, O most beautiful among women? What kind of beloved is your beloved, That thus you adjure us?

She relates his *Qualifications*

[10] "My beloved is dazzling and ruddy, Outstanding among ten thousand. [11] "His head is like gold, pure gold; His locks are like clusters of dates And black as a raven. [12] "His eyes are like doves Beside streams of water, Bathed in milk, And reposed in their setting. [13] "His cheeks are like a bed of balsam, Banks of sweet-scented herbs; His lips are lilies Dripping with liquid myrrh. [14] "His hands are rods of gold Set with beryl; His abdomen is carved ivory Inlaid with sapphires. [15] "His legs are pillars of alabaster Set on pedestals of pure gold; His appearance is like Lebanon Choice as the cedars. [16] "His mouth is full of sweetness.

And he is wholly desirable. This is my beloved and this is my friend, O daughters of Jerusalem."

His *Radiance* - *My beloved is dazzling.*

He is *Ruddy*

He is *Rare* – *Outstanding among ten thousands.*

He looks like Royalty - *His head is like gold, pure gold*

He has *Raven* looking hair - *His locks are like clusters of dates and black as a raven.*

His eyes were like doves by the *Rivers* - *His eyes were like doves beside streams of water, bathed in milk and reposed in their setting.*

His *Rugged* beard smelled good - The Message Bible *"His face is rugged, his beard smells like sage."*

His *Reddish* lips are like lilies - *his lips are like lilies, dripping with liquid myrrh*

His *Rippling* muscles - *His hands are rods of gold set with beryl*

His *Ripped* abdomen - *His abdomen is carved ivory inlaid with sapphires.*

His *Robust* legs are - *His legs are pillars of marble set on bases of fine gold.*

His *Rugged* appearance - Message, *"He stands tall, like a cedar, strong and deep-rooted, a rugged mountain of a man.*

He is *Romantic* - *His mouth is full of sweetness*

He is *well-Rounded* in every way - *Yes, he is altogether lovely. This is my beloved, and this is my friend, O daughters of Jerusalem.*

We of course could apply all of this to Jesus Christ!

Her *Queer* Answer

¹ "Where has your beloved gone, O most beautiful among women? Where has your beloved turned, That we may seek him with you?" ² "My beloved has gone down to his garden, To the beds of balsam, To pasture his flock in the gardens And gather lilies. ³ "I am my beloved's and my beloved is mine, He who pastures his flock among the lilies." - If she doesn't know where he is, how does she know

that he had gone to his garden? The mystery - "He was there all the time!"

What is this garden? Nelson Study Bible note, "On the wedding night, the bride presented herself to Solomon as his garden. But he has another garden to tend as well, and it is one in which he also takes great pleasure. This is the "garden" of his work his responsibility as the King of Israel. The flock is the people; the lilies represent the produce of the land. This realization leads to the strong affirmation in the next verse that the husband and wife belong to each other. Another use of the word garden occurs in 6:11, refers to the Shulamites's homeland."

NET note, "This usage of "garden" might be figurative or literal: (1) He went to a real garden for repose. Solomon did, in fact, own a great many gardens (Eccl 2:4-7; 1 Chr 27:27). (2) The "garden" is a figurative description referring either to: (a) the young woman, (b) their sexual love, or (c) Solomon's harem."

Solomon describes his unique *Queen*

⁴ Dear, dear friend and lover, you're as beautiful as Tirzah, city of delights, Lovely as Jerusalem, city of dreams, the ravishing visions of my ecstasy. ⁵ Your beauty is too much for me—I'm in over my head. I'm not used to this! I can't take it in. Your hair flows and shimmers like a flock of goats in the distance streaming down a hillside in the sunshine. ⁶ Your smile is generous and full— expressive and strong and clean. ⁷ Your veiled cheeks are soft and radiant. ⁸ There's no one like her on earth, never has been, never will be. ⁹ She's a woman beyond compare. My dove is perfection, Pure and innocent as the day she was born, and cradled in joy by her mother. Everyone who came by to see her exclaimed and admired her— All the fathers and mothers, the neighbors and friends, blessed and praised her: ¹⁰ "Has anyone ever seen anything like this— dawn-fresh, moon-lovely, sun-radiant, ravishing as the night sky with its galaxies of stars?" Song of Songs 6:4-10 (MSG)

A *Quiet* time in the garden

¹¹ "I went down to the orchard of nut trees To see the blossoms of the valley, To see whether the vine had budded Or the pomegranates had bloomed. ¹² "Before I was aware, my soul set me Over the chariots of my noble people." ¹³ "Come back, come back, O Shulammite…

A *ReQuest* to gaze upon the Shulamite

Come back, come back, that we may gaze at you!" "Why should you gaze at the Shulammite, As at the dance of the two companies? - I would say, when the Spirit of God moves - join Him!

CHAPTER FIVE

CONQUEST OF LOVE

Him: 1Your feet are so beautiful, perfectly fitted in sandals, noble daughter!* Your sculpted thighs are like jewels, the work of a master hand. 2Your hidden place is open to me like a goblet, perfect and round, that never runs dry of blended wine; Your waist is a mound of wheat— curved and white and fertile— encircled by lilies. 3Your breasts are like two fawns, twins of a gazelle. 4Your neck is as stunning as an ivory tower; your eyes shimmer like the pools in Heshbon by the gate of Bath-rabbim. Your nose is strong and proud like the tower of Lebanon, which points toward Damascus. 5Your head is as stately as Mount Carmel; your hair shines like a tapestry of royal purple cloth— the king is held captive by your locks. 6How beautiful you are, my love, and how pleasing In all your delightful and satisfying ways. 7Your stature is as elegant as a date palm tree, and your breasts are sweet, attractive, and round like clusters of its fruit. 8I say, "I will climb the palm tree; I will take hold of its fruit." May your breasts be like clusters of grapes, the fragrance of your mouth* like fresh apples, 9and may your kisses satisfy like the best wine. **Her**: May the wine go down smoothly for my love, flowing gently over his lips and teeth.* 10I belong to my love, and he has desire for me. (to him) 11Come out into the fields, my love, and there spend the night in the villages. 12Let's rise with the morning and go to the vineyards to see if the vines have budded, If their blossoms have opened, and if the pomegranates are in bloom. There I will give you my love. 13The mandrakes send out their seductive fragrance, and the finest fruits wait at our doors— New pleasures as well as old— I have stored them up for you, my lover.

Her (to him): 1If only you were like my brother, my love, nursed at my mother's breast! Then we could show our affection in public. I would kiss you, and no one would think anything of it. Nobody would look down on me. 2I would take you by the hand and bring you to my mother's house— she has taught me to be a woman. I would give you spiced wine to drink, and you could enjoy the juice of my pomegranates. 3His left hand cradles my head, and his right hand reaches out to embrace me. 4(to the young women of Jerusalem) Heed my warning: I charge you not to excite your love until it is ready. Don't stir a fire in your heart too soon, until it is ready to be satisfied.

Young Women of Jerusalem: 5Who is this woman coming up from the desert, leaning on her love?

Her: Under the apple tree I roused your love for me, in the place where your mother conceived you, in the place where she gave birth to you. 6Set me as a seal over your heart; wear me as an emblem on your arm For love is as strong as death, and jealousy is as relentless as the grave. Love flares up like a blazing fire, a very ardent flame. 7No amount of water can quench love; a raging flood cannot drown it out. If a person tried to exchange all of his wealth for love, then he would be surely rejected. Young **Women of Jerusalem**: 8We have a little sister whose breasts have not yet developed. How shall we protect her until the time when she is spoken for? 9If she is a wall, we will build silver towers of protection; If she is a door, we will barricade the door with the strongest cedar.

Her: 10I was a wall, and now my breasts are like towers; At that time I found completeness and satisfaction in his eyes. 11Solomon had a vineyard in Baal-hamon; he let farmers tend it and charged each a ransom for its produce— 1,000 pieces of silver. 12My vineyard is my own— mine to lend or mine to lease. Solomon, you may have your 1,000; Those who tend the fruit, your 200.

Him: 13You who dwell in the gardens, whose friends are always attentive to your voice, Let me hear it.
Her: 14Come quickly, my love. Be like a gazelle or young stag on the mountains of spices.

Henry Drummond, "Love is life. To love abundantly is to live forever. Why do you want to live tomorrow? It is because there is someone who loves you, and whom you want to see and be with and love back. It is when a man has no one to love him that he commits suicide."

Of course the greatest meaning in time and eternity is the fact that God loves us.

Love always *Expresses* itself

¹ "How beautiful are your feet in sandals, O prince's daughter! The curves of your hips are like jewels, The work of the hands of an artist. ² "Your navel is like a round goblet Which never lacks mixed wine; Your belly is like a heap of wheat Fenced about with lilies. ³ "Your two breasts are like two fawns, Twins of a gazelle. ⁴ "Your neck is like a tower of ivory, Your eyes like the pools in Heshbon By the gate of Bath-rabbim; Your nose is like the tower of Lebanon, Which faces toward

Damascus. ⁵ "Your head crowns you like Carmel, And the flowing locks of your head are like purple threads; The king is captivated by your tresses. ⁶ "How beautiful and how delightful you are, My love, with all your charms! ⁷ "Your stature is like a palm tree, And your breasts are like its clusters. ⁸ "I said, 'I will climb the palm tree, I will take hold of its fruit stalks.' Oh, may your breasts be like clusters of the vine, And the fragrance of your breath like apples, ⁹ And your mouth like the best wine!" "It goes down smoothly for my beloved, Flowing gently through the lips of those who fall asleep.

He praises her beginning with her *Feet* (7:1a)

Song of Sol. 7:1 (a) By this we are taught that our walk must be made safe and comfortable, as well as beautiful and attractive through the death of our Savior. Shoes are made from the hide of a dead animal. So our natural walk must be covered over with the life of our lovely Lord, so that we may "walk with the Lord in the light of His Word." [A Dictionary of Bible Types]

He praises her *Form* (7:1b-4a)

Her *Bodily* curves

This adjective is derived from the verb chāmaq (HED #2665), "to turn." A Mishnaic noun refers to a piece of wood, presumably round (describing pins). In its lone biblical context, the adjective is used to describe the thighs of the beloved, as though they were crafted by craftsmen (SS 7:1). Curvature of thighs is interpreted by a number of cultures as being desirable for child bearing, although here the attribute seems to be purely aesthetic.Complete Biblical Library Hebrew-English Dictionary - The Complete Biblical Library Hebrew-English Dictionary

Her *Belly-button* (7:2a)

Her *Belly*

"Your navel is a round mixing bowl — may it never lack mixed wine! Your belly is a mound of wheat, encircled by lilies." Song of Songs 7:2 (NET1)

Alternately, "your waist." The term בִּטְנֵךְ (bitnekh) probably refers to the woman's "belly" rather than "waist." It is associated with a woman's abdominal/stomach region rather than her hips (Prov 13:25; 18:20; Ezek 3:3). The comparison of her belly to a heap of wheat is visually appropriate because of the similarity of their symmetrical shape and tannish color. The primary point of comparison, however, is based upon the commonplace association of wheat in Israel, namely, wheat was the main staple of the typical Israelite meal (Deut 32:14; 2 Sam 4:6; 17:28; 1 Kgs 5:25; Pss 81:14; 147:14). Just as wheat satisfied an Israelite's physical hunger, she satisfied his sexual hunger. J. S. Deere makes this point in the following manner: "The most obvious commonplace of wheat was its function, that is, it served as one of the main food sources in ancient Palestine. The Beloved was both the 'food' (wheat) and 'drink' (wine) of the Lover. Her physical expression of love nourished and satisfied him. His satisfaction was great for the 'mixed wine' is intoxicating and the 'heap of wheat' was capable of feeding many. The 'heap of wheat' also suggests the harvest, an association which contributes to the emotional quality of the metaphor. The harvest was accompanied with a joyous celebration over the bounty yielded up by the land. So also, the

Beloved is bountiful and submissive in giving of herself, and the source of great joy" ("Song of Solomon," BKCOT, 203-204). [NET Bible]

Her *Breast* (7:3)

Breast

Like many other body parts, the breast has strong symbolic significance in Scripture. The breast is used as an image of female sexuality. The picture of the mother feeding her child at the breast is widely used as a symbol of both comfort and security. The concept of security is also picked up in the protection afforded to the exposed and vulnerable breast by the use of the breastplate as body armor. Almost all uses of the term in Scripture relate directly or indirectly to one of these three concepts. Solomon extols the qualities of the breasts of the beloved woman (Song 4:5; 7:3; 8:10). Proverbs encourages the young man to restrict his sexual activities to his own wife: "May her breasts satisfy you at all times" (Prov 5:19). On the one hand, the images convey a very positive attitude toward the pleasures and comforts of sex as God-given; and on the other hand, a clear condemnation of promiscuous behavior as a misuse of sex. Hosea longs for his wife to "put away ... her adultery from between her breasts" (Hos 2:2 NRSV).

The picture of a little baby comforted and nourished at the mother's breast is evocative for all people and particularly significant for both the mother and the child. For the mother, having children at the breast provides both fulfillment and status: "Who would ever have said ... that Sarah would nurse children?" (Gen 21:7 NRSV); "Blessed [are] ... the breasts that nursed you" (Lk 11:27). But two images present the extremes: dry breasts are synonymous with childlessness (Hos 9:13; see Barrenness) and the proverb "The leech has two daughters; 'Give, give,' they cry" may allude to the frustration of nursing twins (Prov 30:15 NRSV).

For the child there is safety ("safe on my mother's breast" [Ps 22:9]), security ("Can a woman forget her nursing child?" [Is 49:15]) and consolation at the mother's breast. It may be that for the adult, the hug provides a similar comfort. Perhaps it is not stretching the imagination too much to see John's reclining on the breast of Jesus at the Last Supper in those terms (Jn 13:25, 21:20). Jerusalem, like all large cities, was viewed as a mother to her inhabitants, who were encouraged to "rejoice with Jerusalem ... that you may nurse and be satisfied from her consoling breast; that you may drink deeply from her glorious bosom" (Is 66:10-11 NRSV). Even the comfort of God is appropriately pictured as that of a nursing mother (Is 49:15; 66:13). The same picture is occasionally used positively to emphasize success: "You shall suck the milk of nations, you shall suck the breasts of kings" (Is 60:16 NRSV; cf. 49:23) and negatively to represent danger or lack of security: "Blessed are ... the breasts that never nursed" (Lk 23:29 NRSV; cf. Job 3:12; 24:9; Mt 24:19). Beating the breast graphically symbolizes loss of security, or lack of peace of (Nahum 2:7; Is 32:12; Lk 18:13; 23:48).

The breast shelters the emotions and the breath of life. For the soldier a breastplate offered some security (see Armor). Metaphorically, the believer is encouraged to find spiritual security by wearing the breastplate of righteousness (Is 59:17; Eph 6:14), or of "faith and love" (1 Thess 5:8). [Dictionary of Biblical Imagery]

Her *Becoming* neck (4a)

In Scripture the neck is sometimes associated with beauty or prosperity, although in itself it is usually less prominent than the jewelry that adorns it (Gen 41:42; Judg 5:30; Prov 1:9). However, in Song of Songs 4:4 and 7:4 the lover praises his beloved's neck itself, rather than the jewelry she wears, making her the focus of his love.

He praises her *Facial features* (4b-6)

Her clear sparkling *Brown* eyes (4b)

The eyes were regarded as a source of beauty (1 Sam 16:12; Song 1:15; 4:1, 9; 5:12; 6:5; 7:4).

Her *Big* nose (4c)

Your neck is carved ivory, curved and slender. Your eyes are wells of light, deep with mystery. Quintessentially feminine! Your profile turns all heads, commanding attention. Song of Songs 7:4 (MSG)

Her head is *Breathtaking* (5)

You hold your head as high as Mount Carmel. Your dangling curls are royal beauty. Your flowing locks could hold a king captive. Song of Songs 7:5 (GW)

She is delightful to *Behold* (6)

[Groom] How beautiful and charming you are, my love, with your elegance. Song of Songs 7:6 (GW)

She has good *Breath* (8b-9)

8 I say, "I'm going to climb that palm tree! I'm going to caress its fruit!" Oh yes! Your breasts will be clusters of sweet fruit to me, Your breath clean and cool like fresh mint, 9 your tongue and lips like the best wine. Yes, and yours are, too—my love's kisses flow from his lips to mine. Song of Songs 7:8-9 (MSG)

He *Focus* on one of his *Favorite* spots (7-9)

Breasts are mentioned 8 times in this little book! She is stacked and stately! A summary statement - *I am my beloved's, And his desire is for me.* A beautiful picture of how the Lord expresses His love for us. "It is a wonderful thing to know that the Lord has far more delight in His people than we ourselves have ever had in Him. Some day we shall enjoy Him to the fullest; some day He will be everything to us; but as long as we are here, we never appreciate Him as much as He appreciates us." [Ironside]

They want to express their love by *Finding* a romantic getaway place

11 *"Come, my beloved, let us go out into the country, Let us spend the night in the villages.* 12 *"Let us rise early and go to the vineyards;*

Let us see whether the vine has budded And its blossoms have opened, And whether the pomegranates have bloomed. There I will give you my love. ¹³ "The mandrakes have given forth fragrance; And over our doors are all choice fruits, Both new and old, Which I have saved up for you, my beloved.

"They want to get away to the countryside, to find some privacy. They will lodge, that is, spend the night somewhere...where she will give herself completely to her lover. The giving off of fragrance is another reference to the early spring season, when the flowers are in bloom."

"The woman now invites her lover to a trip in the countryside. The countryside is a location of intimacy. Thus, the invitation to the countryside is an invitation to lovemaking. Her purpose is to spend some time in the countryside with her lover for the purpose of physical intimacy. She continues her invitation to the man by urging him to rise early and go into the countryside. It is a way of emphasizing that she desires to spend as much time as possible in his presence. The reference to the vineyards, can be used to refer both to the woman's body and to the place of lovemaking, perhaps at times echoing with both meaning." [The New International Commentary of the O.T.]

She wants to express her love *Freely* (8:1-4)

1 "Oh that you were like a brother to me Who nursed at my mother's breasts. If I found you outdoors, I would kiss you; No one would despise me, either. 2 "I would lead you and bring you Into the house of my mother, who used to instruct me; I would give you spiced wine to drink from the juice of my pomegranates. 3 "Let his left hand be under my head And his right hand embrace me." 4 "I want you to swear, O daughters of Jerusalem, Do not arouse or awaken my love Until she pleases."

In that culture it was acceptable for brothers and sisters to show affection for one another in public. It was not acceptable for husband and wife to show such affection publicly.

The point is this, love is designed to be expressed, often the longer one is married, the less love is expressed. But this should be the other way around. God's love is always being expressed and that love motivates us upward and onward.

Love always *Experiences* obstacles (8:5)

"Who is this coming up from the wilderness leaning on her beloved?" "Beneath the apple tree I awakened you; There your mother was in labor with you, There she was in labor and gave you birth.

Of course the one coming up from the wilderness is Solomon and his wife. The wilderness is often a type of trial and difficulty. Every married couple will sooner or later face storms of life. The experience of the little foxes that seek to ruin the vineyard; they had experienced the time of broken fellowship; and the searching; etc.

leaning on her beloved - we don't have to face trials alone!

As one put it, "Who is this that cometh up from the wilderness leaning upon her beloved?" Her posture then is that of "leaning." His relation to her is that of a divine supporter. What does this leaning mean? Why, first of all, there can be no leaning on another unless we believe in that other's presence and nearness. A man does not lean on a staff which is not in his hand, nor on a friend of whose presence he is not aware...Leaning also implies nearness. We cannot lean on that which is far off and unapproachable. Now, it is a delightful help to us in believing repose if we can understand that Christ is not only with us, but to an intense degree near us...Leaning now becomes easy. To lean implies the throwing of one's weight from one's self on to another, and this is the Christian's life. The first act that made him a Christian at all, was when the whole weight of his sin was laid on Christ. When by faith the sinner ceased to carry his own burden, but laid that burden on the great Substitute's shoulder, it was that leaning which made him a Christian. In proportion as he learns this lesson of casting all his burden upon his Lord, he will be more and more a Christian; and when he shall have completely unloaded himself, and cast all his matters upon his God, and shall live in the power and strength of God, and not in his own, then shall he have attained to the fullness of the stature of a perfect man in Christ Jesus. To lean, I say, is to throw your weight off from yourself on to another - being fatigued, to make another fatigued if he can be; being wearied, to make another take your weariness, and so yourself to proceed with your load transferred to a substitute. Yes, I repeat it, this is the true Christian life - to leave everything that troubles me with him who loves me better than I love myself; to leave all that depresses me with him whose wisdom and whose power are more than a match for all emergencies. Herein is wisdom, never to try to stand alone by my own strength, never to trust to creatures, for they will fail me if I rest upon them, but to make my ever blessed Lord Christ, in his manhood and in his Godhead, the leaning place of my whole soul, casting every burden upon him who is able to bear it. This is what I think is meant in the text by leaning."

"Child of My love, lean hard,
And let Me feel the pressure of thy care;
I know thy burden, child. I shaped it;
Poised it in Mine Own hand; made no proportion
In its weight to thine unaided strength,
For even as I laid it on, I said,
'I shall be near, and while she leans on Me,
This burden shall be Mine, not hers;
So shall I keep My child within the circling arms
Of My Own love.' Here lay it down, nor fear
To impose it on a shoulder which upholds
The government of worlds. Yet closer come:
Thou art not near enough. I would embrace thy care;

So I might feel My child reposing on My breast.
Thou lovest Me? I knew it. Doubt not then;
But loving Me, lean hard."

Love is *Exacting* (6a)

Put me like a seal over your heart, Like a seal on your arm -Longman, "The seal in mind here is the seal of ownership and personal identification...The woman is asking the man to allow her to own him, but not in some kind of cheap commercial sense; she wants him to willingly give himself to her. She asks him to mark her on his heart and arm...Taken together; heart and arm signify the whole person."

Love *Excels* in strength (6b)

For love is as strong as death - Ogden, "Just as death is powerful and unending, so love is also powerful and unending. Death lasts forever; our love will never die, or Death is very powerful, so is love. Nothing can overcome true love."

"What besides love is so strong as death! With steadfast foot, Death marches over the world. No mountain can restrain the invasion, of this all-conquering king. There is no valley so fair that he does not intrude and stalk. Everywhere and in every place beneath the moon, death holds sway. None among the son's of Adam can withstand Death's insidious advances. When the hour is come, none can bid him delay.

Mightiest among the mighty is death, but Christ's love is strong as death. It too can climb the mountain and march into the valley. Who can stand against it? He will "have mercy on whom He will have mercy." Who can measure the strength of Christ's love? Men have defied it but their defiance has not overcome; they have found it hard to kick against the pricks. One might sooner defy the grace, and hurl back the pale horse of death on its haunches, then turn back the Holy Spirit when He comes in His divine omnipotence to lay hold upon the heart and soul of man. As all the owls and bats with all their hooting could not scare back the sun when once its hour to rise has come; so all the sins of man cannot turn back the light of love, when God decrees that it should shine upon a heart. Death is weakness itself, when compared with, the love of Christ."

Love is *Exclusive* (6c)

Jealousy is as severe as Sheol - Zogbo, "The parallel structure of the sentences indicates that here it has the same sense as love; so it has a positive sense, namely the exclusive devotion they have for each other. "Cruel" is rather misleading. The Hebrew adjective has almost the same sense as "strong" in the previous clause. "Grave" is literally "Sheol" the place of the dead. Our complete devotion binds us just like the grave holds onto the death."

"The idea is that the love of Christ in the form of jealously, is as hard and as relentless, as is the grave and Hades. Hell never loses one of its slaves. Once the iron gate of the grave is shut, there is no escape! Such is the love of Christ - you may sooner unlock Hades and let one of its prisoners free, then you could snatch one of His, out of His hand. You could sooner rob death of its prey, then Jesus of His purchased ones. Just as surely as every lost soul is lost, so every believing soul is saved. God is jealously guarding His exclusive rights to His own children."

Love is *Exciting*

Its flashes are flashes of fire -it can be rendered "love's arrows are fiery!"

Love is a Divine *Expression*

the very flame of the LORD - "A number of scholars, believe the phrase to be two separate words, the second of which is yah. This latter is then interpreted as an abbreviated form of the divine name Yahweh, giving a translation "flame of Yahweh." This text provides the basis for many commentators believe that the Song is not a simple love song, but a treatise on God's love for His people."

"The words like a mighty flame are, literally, "like the very flame of the Lord" (cf. niv marg.). Thus the Lord is portrayed as the Source of this powerful love." [The Bible Knowledge Commentary: An Exposition of the Scriptures by Dallas Seminary Faculty]

Without His love, there would be no love like that being described between a husband and wife. PS: Of all the commentaries I have on this book, which is now over 25 of them, all of them believe that this song depicts God's love for Israel, and by application, Christ love for the church.

Love cannot be *Extinguished*

"Many waters cannot quench love, nor will rivers overflow it;

Spurgeon, "Many waters could no more destroy His love, than it could drown Noah's ark. In fact the ark mounted higher and higher and higher, as the flood waters prevailed; in the same way the love of Christ, seems to rise higher and higher and higher, in proportion to the storms of life. Oh what floods has Christ's love endured - think of the flood of our sins, the many waters of backslidings; the surge of our unbelief - yet it has never failed and we are persuaded that neither life, nor death, nor things present, nor things to come, nor angels. nor principalities, nor powers, nor height, nor depth, nor any other creature shall be able to separate us from the love of God which is in Christ Jesus our Lord."

Love is beyond *Expense*

If a man were to give all the riches of his house for love, It would be utterly despised - You cannot purchase love (1) Because all things are already His! From this little speck we call earth, to the spectrum of the universe - all things are His! (2) If He wanted anything, He could just speak it into existence, and as He did in the first place. (3) Because His love, like His grace cannot be purchased - not with good works; church attendance; baptism; lame promises; etc. Any and all attempts would prove to be futile, it would be utterly despised.

Love is *Exemplary* (8-12)

Here she remembers a day when she was not yet of marriageable age. Her brothers are heard to express their desire to protect her.

Her *Purity*

8 "We have a little sister, And she has no breasts; What shall we do for our sister On the day when she is spoken for? 9 "If she is a wall, We will build on her a battlement of silver; But if she is a door, We will barricade her with planks of cedar." 10 "I was a wall, and my breasts were like towers; Then I became in his eyes as one who finds peace - Baptist Study Bible, "The plan of her brothers depends upon the character of the Shulamite [referring to her youth]. If she is strong as a "wall" in withstanding the advances of her suitors, they will encourage and praise her, but she is a "door" easily entered, they will protect her from advances." Notice verse 10, she declares that she was indeed as a wall.

Her *Generosity*

[11] "Solomon had a vineyard at Baal-hamon; He entrusted the vineyard to caretakers. Each one was to bring a thousand shekels of silver for its fruit. [12] "My very own vineyard is at my disposal; The thousand shekels are for you, Solomon, And two hundred are for those who take care of its fruit." - Nelson Study Bible, "Solomon owned many vineyards...Baal Harmon was a site near Shunem, the town near where the Shulamite may have been raised. It was customary for an absentee owner to lease out a vineyard. As Solomon's vineyard had been entrusted to the Shulamite's brothers, so had the Shulamite. After caring for this vineyard, the brothers, earned one thousand shekels profit. But they also cared for and protected the king's other "vineyard," the Shulamite. Now she requested that her brothers be rewarded with two hundred shekels profit. My own vineyard: this phrase takes us back to 1:6, where the Shulamite makes a play on words with vineyard. Here she sees that vineyard of old, but indicates that she now has another "vineyard" to tend - her dear husband."

Love lives in *Expectancy* (13-14)

¹³ *"O you who sit in the gardens, My companions are listening for your voice— Let me hear it!"* ¹⁴ *"Hurry, my beloved, And be like a gazelle or a young stag On the mountains of spices."* – as one put it, "I think, surely, that this is the result of true love. Does not love always wish to see the object on which its heart is fixed? When your dearest one parts from you for a while, do you not always wish for a speedy return? Where there is great love, there will always be great longing."

One thing cannot be denied, this book is a powerful testimony to the conquering power of love.

In the Valley of the Vision:

"O Father of Jesus,
Help me to approach You with deepest reverence,
not with presumption,
not with cringing fear, but with holy boldness.
You are beyond the grasp of my understanding,
but not beyond that my love…

My heart melts, at the love of Jesus...
He is mine and I am His...
But my love is frost and cold, ice and snow;
Let His love warm me,
lighten my burden,
be my heaven;
Let the mighty tide of His everlasting love
cover the rocks of my sin and care;"

Made in the USA
San Bernardino, CA
27 May 2016